fantastic
FURNITURE

in an afternoon®

fantastic
FURNITURE
in an afternoon®

Mickey Baskett

Sterling Publishing Co., Inc.

New York

Prolific Impressions Production Staff:

Editor: Mickey Baskett
Copy: Phyllis Mueller
Graphics: Dianne Miller, Karen Turpin
Styling: Lenos Key, Kirsten Jones
Photography: Jerry Mucklow
Administration: Jim Baskett

Every effort has been made to insure that the information presented is accurate. Since we have no control over physical conditions, individual skills, or chosen tools and products, the publisher disclaims any liability for injuries, losses, untoward results, or any other damages which may result from the use of the information in this book. Thoroughly read the instructions for all products used to complete the projects in this book, paying particular attention to all cautions and warnings shown for that product to ensure their proper and safe use.

No part of this book may be reproduced for commercial purposes in any form without permission by the copyright holder. The written instructions and design patterns in this book are intended for the personal use of the reader and may be reproduced for that purpose only.

Library of Congress Cataloging-in-Publication Data Available

Acknowledgements

Thanks to **Plaid Enterprises, Inc.** (plaidonline.com) for supplying FolkArt® Acrylic Paints, Stencil Décor Stencils, Stamp Décor foam stamps, FolkArt® Crackle Medium, Royal Coat Decoupage Finish, and FolkArt® Varnish for creating these projects.

(10 9 8 7 6 5 4 3 2 1)

Published by Sterling Publishing Company, Inc.
387 Park Avenue South, New York, N.Y. 10016
Produced by Prolific Impressions, Inc.
160 South Candler St., Decatur, GA 30030
© 2001 by Prolific Impressions, Inc.
Distributed in Canada by Sterling Publishing
c/o Canadian Manda Group, One Atlantic Avenue, Suite 105
Toronto, Ontario, Canada M6K 3E7
Distributed in Great Britain and Europe by Cassell PLC
Wellington House, 125 Strand, London WC2R 0BB, England
Distributed in Australia by Capricorn Link (Australia) Pty. Ltd.
P.O. Box 704, Windsor, NSW 2756 Australia

Printed in USA
All rights reserved
Sterling ISBN 0-8069-2973-1

Contents

Introduction

The projects in this book present an array of techniques for decorating and refurbishing furniture. Most of the projects are easy to do and can be accomplished in an afternoon or a weekend. They range in complexity from simple pieces perfect for beginners that employ color washing, gold leafing, stamping, stenciling, and fabric fixes to more advanced projects that include decorative painting and faux finishing techniques. There are step-by-step instructions and numerous photographs to guide you.

With paint, stain, paper, and fabric, you can give new life to old furniture or transform inexpensive, unfinished pieces into fantastic works of art that you'll enjoy for years. Using furniture pieces you decorated yourself is a rewarding and creative way to add personal touches to the rooms of your home.

Paint a table for a special friend in her favorite colors. Try a stamped design that mimics mosaics; or decorate a tabletop with stenciling, gold leafing, glass etching, or decoupage. Use the motifs from the Chicken Chair to create a coordinating cupboard. Create fun furniture for kids that they'll want to pass on to their own children. Use the ideas presented with each project as a springboard for designing and personalizing. Have fun being your own furniture designer!

Supplies
FOR FURNITURE PREPARATION

◆ *For Cleaning & Stripping*

Mild Detergent or Bubble Bath:

If you are going to paint your piece of furniture, you will find that stripping it is not necessary – just clean it up. To remove dirt, dust, cobwebs, etc., use a cleaner that does not leave a gritty residue. Effective cleaners include **mild dishwashing detergent** and **bubble bath**. Mix the cleaner with water and wash the furniture with a cellulose sponge. Rinse and wipe dry with soft cloth rags.

Paint Thinner:

Use **paint thinner** and a **steel wool pad** to remove waxy buildup on stained wooden pieces and old varnish or shellac.

Paint Stripper:

There are several reasons you may wish to strip a piece of furniture. If you plan to stain, pickle, or color wash the piece, you will need to get down to bare wood. And if the piece of furniture is covered with layers of badly flaking, wrinkled, or uneven paint that can't be sanded smooth, stripping is necessary. There are many brands of paint strippers available at do-it-yourself and hardware stores. Apply **paint stripper** with a brush. When the paint begins to wrinkle and lift, remove it with a **paint scraper**.

◆ *For Sanding & Filling*

Sandpaper:

Sandpaper is available in different grits for different types of sanding. Generally, start with medium grit sandpaper, and then use fine grit to sand before painting. Between coats of paint, sand lightly with fine or extra fine sandpaper.

Sanding Block:

This wooden block that sandpaper is wrapped around aids smooth sanding on flat surfaces.

Electric Sander:

A handheld **electric finishing sander** aids in sanding large, flat areas. Use wet/dry sandpaper and wet it to keep down dust. Wipe away sanding dust with a **tack cloth**.

Wood Filler:

Wood filler or wood putty, applied with a **putty knife**, is used to fill cracks, holes, dents, and nicks for a smooth, even painting surface. You can use wood filler on raw wood furniture or previously painted or stained furniture. Let dry and sand smooth.

◆ *For Priming & Base Painting*

Primer:

A **primer** fills and seals wood and helps paint to bond properly. A **stain blocking primer** keeps an old finish from bleeding through new paint. This is especially necessary if you have a dark piece of furniture and want to paint it a light color. Always allow primer to dry thoroughly before base painting.

You can make your own primer by slightly thinning white flat latex wall paint with water. One coat on an old painted or stained piece helps give the surface some "tooth" so the base paint will adhere properly.

Paint for Base Painting:

Base paint is the first layer of paint applied to a surface after a primer. Base paint your furniture piece with **latex wall paint in an eggshell or satin finish, acrylic indoor/outdoor paint**, or **acrylic craft paint**. Brush on the paint, using long, smooth strokes. Work carefully to avoid runs, drips, or sags.

All the painting in this book was done with waterbase paints. Today's formulas provide as much wear-and-tear protection as oil-based paints.

Brushes:

Base paint can be applied with a **foam brush** or **bristle paint brush**. For painting details or smaller areas, use a 1" **craft brush**. For painting larger flat areas, a **foam roller** is a good choice.

Miscellaneous Supplies:

Wear **latex gloves** to protect your hands from cleaners, solvents, and paints. These tight-fitting gloves, available at hardware stores, paint stores, and home improvement centers, will not impair your dexterity.

Masking Tape:

This often under-valued supply is essential for furniture decorating. Use **masking tape** to mask off areas for painting, to make crisp lines, and to protect previously painted areas.

Pictured clockwise at right, beginning at bottom left: 1" craft brush, 2" foam brush, 1-1/2" bristle brush, foam roller, acrylic indoor/outdoor paint, paint thinner, steel wool, latex gloves, paint scraper, paint remover, stain blocking primer, masking tape in a tape dispenser, handheld electric sander, sandpaper, sanding block, putty knife, wood filler, cellulose sponge, soft cloth rag, liquid detergent.

Preparation
OLD FURNITURE TO BE PAINTED

Chances are there's a piece of furniture that's languished for years in your attic, basement, or garage that's a perfect candidate for painting. Tag and yard sales and used furniture stores are other good sources of old furniture. When selecting an old furniture piece, choose one in sound condition. If the legs are wobbly or the drawers stick, make repairs before painting. Repair loose joints with wood glue. If extensive repairs are needed, seek the services of a professional.

When an old piece of furniture is to receive a painted finish, very often all the piece needs is cleaning and sanding. A primer coat may be necessary if the piece has a glossy finish. If the finish is in very bad condition or the varnish is wrinkled and chipped, you may choose to strip it. Stripping is usually a last resort.

A good rule of thumb is to work with what you have. If your old piece of furniture has a dark finish, perhaps you'll decide to paint it dark green to minimize the amount of preparation you'll need to do, instead of trying to cover up the dark finish with a light paint color. Study your piece to determine how much preparation needs to be done.

Step 1 - Removing Hardware

Before cleaning or sanding, remove all hardware, such as door and drawer pulls. (**photo 1**) Depending upon your piece and what you're planning to do, it also may be necessary to remove hinges, doors, drawers, or mirrors. This is also the time to remove upholstered seats from chairs. Drawer pulls and knobs should be painted or treated while they are detached.

Precautions & Tips

- Read product labels carefully and observe all manufacturer's recommendations and cautions.

- **Always** work in a well-ventilated area or outdoors.

- Wear gloves to protect your hands.

- Wear a dust mask or respirator to protect yourself from dust and fumes.

- Use a piece of old or scrap vinyl flooring for a work surface. Vinyl flooring is more protective and more convenient than layers of newspaper or plastic sheeting. Paint or finishes can seep through newspapers, and newspapers always get stuck to your shoes. Plastic sheeting is slippery. Spills can be wiped up quickly from vinyl, and nothing will seep through it to your floor. Small pieces of vinyl can be purchased inexpensively as remnants at floor covering stores and building supply centers.

- Dispose of solvents properly. If in doubt of how to dispose of them, contact your local government for instructions. Do not pour solvents or paint strippers down drains or toilets.

Photo 1 - Removing hardware.

Step 2 - Cleaning

The next step is removing accumulated dust, grease, and grime. Sometimes careful cleaning is all that's needed before painting. To clean, mix a little mild detergent or bubble bath with water in a bucket or basin. Using a household sponge, wash the piece with the soapy solution. (**photo 2**). Rinse with clear water. Wipe the piece with soft cloth rags to remove surface water. Allow to air dry until the piece is completely dry.

If your piece has years of wax buildup or is covered with shellac or varnish that has cracked or worn unevenly, use a solvent to provide a thorough cleaning. This is necessary because wax repels waterbased paints and shellac and varnish are poor undercoats for paint. Pour a solvent such as paint thinner, mineral spirits, or a liquid sandpaper

Photo 2 - Washing a piece with a mild soapy solution.

Photo 3 - Removing wax buildup with a steel wool pad dipped in paint thinner.

product in a metal can or enamel bowl. Dip a steel wool pad in the solvent and rub the surface (**photo 3**). Rinse the pad in solvent occasionally as you work, and replace the solvent in your container when it gets dirty. When you're finished, allow the piece to air dry.

Step 3 - Sanding

An important step in the preparation process, sanding dulls the old finish so new paint will adhere properly and creates a smooth surface for painting. To sand the piece smooth, start with medium grit sandpaper, then use fine grit. Always sand in the direction of the grain. Wrap the sandpaper around a sanding block on flat surfaces (**photo 4**). Use a handheld electric finishing sander on larger flat areas, such as tops and shelves (**photo 5**). Hold the paper in your hand when working in tight areas or on curves (**photo 6**). Wipe away dust with a tack cloth. To remove sanding dust from crevices and tight areas, use a brush or a vacuum cleaner.

TIPS:
- When sanding old paint that may contain lead, use wet/dry sandpaper and wet the paper while sanding to prevent creating dust.
- **Always** wear a mask when sanding to prevent inhaling dust.

Photo 4 - Sanding a flat surface with sandpaper wrapped around a sanding block.

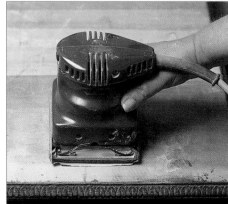

Photo 5 - Sanding a flat surface with a handheld electric finishing sander.

Photo 6 - Sanding in a tight area.

Step 4 - Filling and Smoothing

Fill cracks, dents, nicks, and holes with a paste wood filler or wood putty. Apply the paste with a putty knife, smoothing the material as much as possible and removing any excess before it dries. Follow manufacturer's recommendations regarding drying time. If necessary, apply a second time and let dry thoroughly. Sand smooth when dry. Wipe away dust.

Step 5 - Priming or Undercoating

Priming or undercoating seals the wood and prevents dark areas from showing through a light colored base paint. Don't use a primer if you intend to apply a stain or color wash. And if you're planning to create a distressed finish that involves sanding through the layers of paint or that will reveal some of the bare wood, don't use primer.

For most finishes, flat white latex wall paint that has been diluted with a little water is an appropriate primer. Mix the paint with a little water (about 10%) to make it go on smoothly.

If your piece has a dark stained or varnished surface, apply a stain blocking white primer so the dark stain or varnish won't bleed through your new paint. Stain blocking primers are also available as sprays.

To make your own stain blocking primer, mix equal amounts of white latex wall paint and acrylic varnish. Sponge this mixture over the surface of your piece.

Allow primer to dry overnight. Sand again, lightly, for a smooth surface. Wipe away dust. You're ready to paint!

Step 6 - Base Painting

The base paint is the foundation upon which you build your decorative effects – you can sponge over it, rag it, add decorative painted elements, distress it, or antique it. Because it is your foundation, you want it to be smooth and to have thoroughly covered the old paint or finish.

An eggshell finish acrylic paint is best for your basepaint. A latex wall paint is acceptable for this. Gloss finish paint should not be used when doing decorative effects on top of your basepaint.

Apply base paint with a small roller or a wide fine-bristled brush. Apply one light coat and allow it to dry. Sand with fine sandpaper to smooth the surface. Apply a second coat and allow it to dry thoroughly. If any of the old finish still shows, apply a third coat. Allow to dry. You are now ready to enjoy your piece or to add additional decorative effects. ❏

Photo 7 - Filling a crack with wood putty.

Photo 8 - Applying white primer with a bristle paint brush.

Photo 9 - Base painting after primer.

OPTIONAL: STRIPPING

Furniture that was previously painted doesn't need stripping if the finish is sound and not too thick. However, if the existing paint or varnish is chipped, blistered, or cracked, or if the original finish was poorly applied, or if the paint on the piece is so thick it's obscuring the lines or details of the piece, stripping is warranted. You can, of course, have the stripping done by a professional – all you'll need to do is sand the piece afterward. Sometimes it costs less to have a professional do the job than it would to buy the supplies and equipment to do the job yourself.

If you wish to strip the piece yourself, purchase a liquid, gel, or paste product specifically made for the job you're doing. (These generally are labeled "stripper" or "paint remover" and may be waterbased or solvent-based.) Read the label carefully and follow the instructions exactly. Work in a well-ventilated space and wear gloves, goggles, and protective clothing.

Photo 1 - Applying the stripper with a bristle brush.

Step 1 - Applying the Stripper

Apply an even layer of stripper to the surface with a bristle brush (**photo 1**) in the direction of the grain of the wood. Wait the recommended amount of time. The old paint or finish will soften, look wrinkled, and start to lift. Be patient! Chemical strippers give the best results when you allow them enough time to work properly.

Step 2 - Removing the Old Finish

Use a paint scraper to lift the old finish from the surface (**photo 2**), again working in the direction of the grain. Be careful not to gouge or scrape the surface as you work. On curves, in crevices, and on carved areas, remove the old finish with steel wool, an old bristle brush, toothpicks, or rags.

Photo 2 - Lifting the softened old finish with a paint scraper.

FINISHING YOUR PROJECT

If you haven't used indoor/outdoor paint for your decorating, you will want to give your finished piece a protective coating. Varnishes and sealers are available in a variety of finishes – matte, satin, and gloss. Satin is my favorite. It gives a nice luster but doesn't emphasize uneven brush strokes like a gloss finish can.

Use waterbase varnishes and sealers that are compatible with acrylic paints for sealing and finishing. They are available in brush on and spray formulations. Choose products that are non-yellowing and quick drying.

Apply the finish according to the manufacturer's instructions. Several thin coats are better than one thick coat (**photo 3**). Let dry between coats according to the manufacturer's recommendations. A furniture piece such as a breakfast table, which will receive a lot of use, will need more coats of sealer or varnish for protection than a piece that is decorative or receives less use.

Photo 3: - Applying waterbase varnish with a foam brush.

Preparation
NEW, UNFINISHED WOOD FURNITURE

New unfinished wood furniture requires less preparation than old furniture – often sanding and priming are all that's necessary.

Step 1 - Sanding

Sand the furniture with fine grit sandpaper, sanding with the grain of the wood, to remove rough edges and smooth the surface. Use a sanding block (**photo 1**) or handheld electric sander on flat surfaces. Hold the paper in your hand on curved areas. Remove dust with a tack cloth or a dry dust cloth. Don't use a damp cloth – the dampness could raise the grain of the wood.

On some furniture, glue may have seeped out of the joints. It's important to remove any glue residue – paint won't adhere to it. If possible, sand away the dried glue. If sanding doesn't remove it, scrape it lightly with a craft knife.

Photo 1 - Sanding with a sanding block.

Step 2 - Sealing (optional)

If there are knots or dark places on the piece, seal them with clear sealer or shellac (**photo 2**). Let dry completely. This will keep sap or residue from bleeding through the base paint.

Photo 2 - Sealing with shellac.

Photo 3 - Applying a primer.

Why Choose Waterbase Paints?

Because waterbase paints have so many advantages and are so readily available, they were used for all the projects in this book. Some advantages include:

• They have less odor because they contain far less solvent than oil-base paints, and so are much less apt to provoke headache or nausea. Some types are considered non-toxic.

• Cleanup is easy with soap and water, so the painter is not exposed to solvents in the cleaning of tools or brushes.

• They are safer to use indoors and not nearly as polluting as solvent based paints in their manufacturing process or in the volatile organic compounds (VOCs) they release after application.

Step 3 - Filling (optional)

If your piece has nail holes, gaps, or cracks, fill them with wood filler or wood putty, using a putty knife. Smooth the material as much as possible and remove any excess before it dries. Follow manufacturer's recommendations regarding drying time. When dry, sand smooth. Wipe away dust.

Step 4 - Priming

Paint the piece with a coat of diluted flat white latex wall paint (mixed by adding about 10% water to paint) or spray primer (**photo 3**). Let dry thoroughly. Sand with fine sandpaper. Wipe away dust with a tack cloth.

Step 5 - Base Painting

Apply base paint with a small roller or a wide fine-bristled brush. Apply one light coat and allow it to dry. Sand with fine sandpaper to smooth the surface. Apply a second coat and allow it to dry thoroughly. If any of the old finish still shows, apply a third coat. Allow to dry. You are now ready to enjoy your piece or to add additional decorative effects.

Furniture
DECORATING

The projects in this book are examples of the many techniques you can use to decorate furniture:

- *Color Washing/Staining*
- *Crackling*
- *Decoupage*
- *Design Painting*
- *Distressing*
- *Fabric Fixes*
- *Glass Etching*
- *Gold Leafing*
- *Solid Color Painting*
- *Sponging*
- *Stamping*
- *Stenciling*

The techniques are easy to accomplish and inexpensive to complete. Step-by-step instructions, numerous photographs, and patterns are provided.

Many types and styles of furniture – old and new and in-between, fanciful and formal, large and small – are represented in these projects. The designs can be adapted to fit a variety of furniture pieces and for multiple uses. Create them as they are presented for beautiful, proven results or use the ideas, techniques, and motifs to create your own inspired treasures, choosing furniture pieces and colors to suit your decor and color schemes. The finished results will express your style, enliven your rooms, and earn admiration and compliments from your family and friends. ❏

Color Washing/Staining

Color staining imparts vibrant hues to wood while allowing the grain and natural characteristics of the wood to show through. The technique can be used to create designs or to create backgrounds for stained, stenciled, stamped or painted designs. Simply brush on the stain and wipe away the excess — that's it.

A variety of pre-mixed products are available for color staining, but it's easy to create custom colors by mixing neutral glazing medium with acrylic craft paint, latex paint, or paint glaze.

The technique shown in the photos uses two colors of stain to create a design that resembles parquet. It is accomplished by using a contact-type paper and cutting away areas of the design.

BASIC SUPPLIES

Options:
- Acrylic paint, or latex paint, to create a stain mixed with neutral glazing medium
- Acrylic stain
- Oil-based stain
- Sponge brush or bristle brush, for applying stain
- Soft cloth rags, to wipe away excess stain and buff surfaces

HERE'S HOW

1. Stain the entire piece with the lightest color first. Allow to dry. (**photo 1**)
2. Create designs by taping off or using a stencil. Here a contact-type paper was applied to the entire surface. The design was transferred to the paper, then areas were cut away where the darker stain was desired.(**photo 2**)
3. Stain with the darker color. (**photo 3**). Peeling away the paper reveals the two colors of stain.

Photo 1. Staining with a lighter color.

Photo 2. Taping off area for staining with a darker color.

Photo 3. Creating a design by staining with a darker color.

ANIMAL PRINT TABLE

Created by Kirsten Jones

Two wood-tone stain colors create an animal print design on the top of this console table. To create the design, masking tape was used to cover the tabletop. The design was transferred to the tape, and a craft knife was used to carefully cut out the design. Be careful not to cut too deeply – you don't want to mark the tabletop.

SUPPLIES

Furniture Piece:
Wooden console table

Stain:
Oak gel stain, 8 oz.
Walnut gel stain, 8 oz.

Tools & Other Supplies:
Spray polyurethane finish, satin sheen
Staining pads
Masking tape, 3" wide (or contact-type paper)
Craft knife
Transfer paper

INSTRUCTIONS

Preparation:
1. Prepare wood surface for staining, following instructions in the "Furniture Preparation" section.
2. Trace pattern. Enlarge as needed to fit your table.

Staining:
1. Stain entire table with oak stain, following manufacturer's instructions. (Oak is the lighter color.) Let dry.
2. Apply masking tape to entire tabletop, overlapping tape to be sure the top is completely covered.
3. Transfer pattern to masking tape on tabletop, repeating pattern to cover entire tabletop.
4. Using a craft knife, carefully cut out animal print pattern. Do not press so hard that you cut into the table – cut only the tape. Remove tape from cutout areas.
5. Stain open areas of tabletop with walnut (the darker color) stain. Let dry.
6. Remove tape. Let dry completely.

Finishing:
Seal with polyurethane spray, following manufacturer's instructions. ❏

Pattern for Animal Print Table
Enlarge @118% or size to fit your table.

Crackling

*The age and character that naturally comes from years of wind and weather can be easily created on painted surfaces with crackle medium. Crackle medium is a clear liquid. It does not crack, but any waterbased medium (Paint or varnish, for example) applied on top of it reacts by shrinking and forming cracks, creating the distinctive crackled look. There are two ways to create crackled finishes. **One-color crackle** uses latex paint as a basecoat. Crackle medium is applied and allowed to dry. A clear waterbase varnish is used as a topcoat. The crackle medium causes the varnish to form cracks. When dry, the cracks are rubbed with an antiquing medium, which imparts color to the cracks.*
Two-color crackle *uses two latex paint colors — one for the basecoat and one for the topcoat. The crackle medium is applied between the coats of paint, causing the topcoat to crack and reveal the basecoat.*

BASIC SUPPLIES

For One-Color Crackle:
- Latex paint, or acrylic paint, one color
- Crackle medium
- Brush-on clear waterbase varnish
- Antiquing medium or tinted glaze (neutral glazing medium + color)
- Foam brushes

For Two-Color Crackle:
- Latex paint, or acrylic paint, two colors
- Crackle medium
- Foam brushes

HERE'S HOW: ONE-COLOR CRACKLE

Photo 1. Apply the basecoat. Let dry.

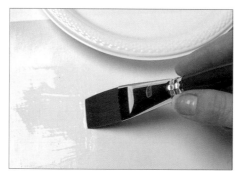

Photo 2. Apply the crackle medium. Let dry. Apply clear varnish atop dried crackle medium. Crack will begin to form as varnish dries.

Photo 3. Apply varnish to darken the cracks.

TWO-COLOR CRACKLE

Photo 1. Apply first paint color. Let dry.

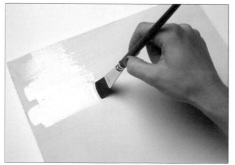

Photo 2. Apply crackle medium. Let dry.

Photo 3. Apply second paint color. Cracks form as paint dries.

CRACKLED LEATHER-LOOK NIGHTSTAND

Created by Kathi Bailey

This nightstand has a crackled top and a coordinating faux leather finish on the legs and sides that's created with a leather texturing tool and tinted glaze. When creating a textured glazed finish, be sure to work one small area at a time so the glaze doesn't dry before you can create the texture.

SUPPLIES

Furniture Piece:
Wooden night table

Paint:
White primer spray
Acrylic paint - brown, black
Neutral glazing medium

Tools & Other Supplies:
Leather texturing tool
Crackle medium
Sandpaper, 220 grit
Acrylic sealer spray
Sponge brushes
Paper palette
Tack cloth
Rags
Masking tape

INSTRUCTIONS

Preparation:
1. Lightly sand entire piece to remove sheen. Wipe off dust and grit with a tack cloth.
2. Spray completely with white primer. Let dry one hour.

Create Leather-Like Texture:
The leather-texture is applied to the entire night stand except the top surface.
1. Paint entire piece with two coats brown. Let dry.
2. You will not do this technique on the top of the nightstand. Place a piece of protective paper and tape in place to mask off tabletop.
3. Mix one part brown paint with three parts neutral glazing medium. Dampen leather texturing tool.
4. Working one area of the table at a time (about one square foot), apply glaze mixture with a sponge brush. Wait 30 seconds to one minute.
5. Pounce leather texturing tool on glaze to remove some the glaze and create texture. **See Photo.** Periodically wipe tool on a rag to remove glaze. Repeat over entire table, except top. Let dry one hour. Reserve remaining glaze.

Crackling:
1. Remove masking from top.
2. Apply crackled medium to top with a sponge brush, following manufacturer's instructions. Let dry.
3. Brush with remaining glaze mixture. Cracks will form. Don't overbrush. Let dry.

Finishing:
1. Paint trim areas with black paint, using photo as a guide. Let dry.
2. Spray with acrylic sealer. ❏

Pictured at left: Pounce leather texturing tool on glaze-coated surface to create the leather-like texture.

Decoupage

Decoupage – the art of cutting or tearing paper designs and applying them to surfaces, then covering with a finish – can be used to add texture, color, and design interest to surfaces. Traditional decoupage was done with glue and layers of varnish. Today's decoupage medium is a clear-drying liquid that is used as both glue and varnish.

BASIC SUPPLIES

- Paper
- Paint for base painting
- Decoupage finish
- Scissors

HERE'S HOW

1. Base paint surface. Let dry.
2. Cut out motifs from paper or fabric with small scissors (**photo 1**) or tear paper into irregular shapes (**photo 2**). Tearing can give an uneven, beveled edge to papers.
3. *Either* apply decoupage medium to the back of cutout motifs with an applicator brush and position on the surface *or* brush decoupage medium on the surface and position paper pieces. (**photo 3**) Let dry.
4. Apply at least two coats of decoupage medium over the paper or fabric to finish. (**photo 4**) Let dry between coats.

Photo 1. Cutting paper with scissors.

Photo 2. Tearing paper to create uneven edges.

Photo 3. Gluing pieces to the surface with decoupage medium.

Photo 4. Applying decoupage finish over the adhered paper.

Handmade Paper-Covered Table

Created by Kathi Bailey

*Beautiful papers, a rubber stamp, and decoupage finish are used to decorate the top
of this table. The torn paper technique is quick and easy.
Handmade paper is available in wonderful colors and textures – find it at art supply and
craft stores (or consider taking a course to learn to make your own paper). You can find
wonderful prints and solid colors of tissue paper – often you can buy individual sheets –
at stores that specialize in gift wrap and party supplies.*

Supplies

Furniture Piece:
Round wooden table on metal base,
   36" diameter

Paper:
Tissue papers - metallic gold, metallic
   copper, purple, turquoise, aqua
Handmade papers - multi-color,
   metallic

Paint:
Acrylic craft paint - gold metallic
   (2 oz.), black
Spray paint - white, black

Tools & Other Supplies:
Rubber stamp with feather motif
Sandpaper, 220 grit
Decoupage finish, 8 oz.
Sponge brushes
Artist's paint brush - #1 round
Tack cloth
Optional: Polyurethane sealer

Instructions

Preparation:
1. Remove tabletop from base if possible, for ease of painting the legs.
2. Clean legs and spray with at least two coats of black paint. Let dry.
3. Clean tabletop and sand lightly to rough up surface. Wipe away dust with a tack cloth.
4. Spray tabletop with two coats white paint. Let dry one hour.

Decoupaging:
1. Rip and tear tissue paper and handmade paper into uneven shapes.
2. Use a sponge brush to apply decoupage medium to the tabletop, and adhere pieces of paper randomly, using photo as a guide. The brush, loaded with finish can be pounced on top of the paper to smooth it into place.
3. Apply one coat decoupage medium to entire tabletop to seal. Let dry thoroughly.

Stamping & Painting:
1. Stamp feather randomly on tabletop with black paint. Let dry 10 minutes. See "Here's How" in the "Stamping" section for information on loading stamps.
2. Highlight feathers, using round brush and gold metallic paint. Let dry 30 minutes.

Finishing:
1. Apply two coats decoupage medium to entire tabletop. Let dry between coats. Let cure 48 hours before use.
2. *Option:* If table is to receive hard use or be used for serving food or beverages, apply polyurethane sealer for additional protection. ❏

Design Painting

Painted designs are a way to create a coordinated, custom look on furniture, and the designs on the following pages show just how versatile painted designs can be. Patterns are included for all the designs; they can be enlarged or reduced as needed to fit your surface. Acrylic craft paints, which were used to paint the designs, come in a wide array of pre-mixed colors and they are easy to use, even for beginners. Find them at craft stores or craft departments.

BASIC SUPPLIES

- Acrylic craft paint
- Artist's paint brushes - rounds, liners, and flats in various sizes
- Tracing paper and pencil
- Transfer paper and stylus
- Palette or disposable foam plate

HERE'S HOW

1. Prepare furniture piece according to the instructions in the "Furniture Preparation" section.
2. Base paint piece.
3. Trace design pattern from book on tracing paper. (**photo 1**) Enlarge or reduce pattern to fit, if needed.
4. Transfer design to surface, using transfer paper and a stylus. (**photo 2**)
5. Paint the design.

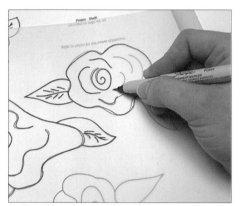

Photo 1. Tracing the pattern.

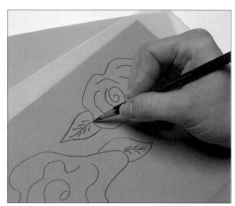

Photo 2. Transferring design to surface.

Photo 3. Lifting the paper reveals the transferred design, ready for painting.

Tips for Successful Decorative Painting

- Use the largest brush you can handle that fits the area of the design you're painting.

- Use round or flat brushes for applying color, flat brushes for blending, shading and highlighting, and liner brushes for painting details and outlining.

Painting Terms:

Washing - When brushed on a surface, a washing creates a thin veil of color. A wash is achieved by diluting paint with water.

Shading - Shading creates shadows, darkens and deepens color, and makes an area recede. In decorative painting, one side of painted subject is often shaded to add depth and dimension.

Highlighting - Highlighting creates dimension by adding light in the form of a lighter color and makes an area seem closer.

Outlining - Outlining, usually done with a liner brush, adds emphasis to designs. Outlining also may be done with a fine tip permanent marker.

BEEHIVE TABLE

Created by Susan Fouts-Kline

This fanciful table is decorated with a stylized bee skep and bright flowers. Dots, checks, and sections of vibrant color help make it a charming accent piece. The painting style is very simple, yet creates sensational results. This design can be painted on chairs, chests, any piece that you want to give a new life.

SUPPLIES

Furniture Piece:
Wooden end table with rectangular top and turned legs, 8-1/2" x 11"

Acrylic Craft Paint:
Black
Butter pecan
Clay bisque
French blue
Heather
Lavender
Lemon
Light blue
Pastel green
Peach
Rose pink
White

Artist's Paint Brushes:
Wash - #1
Shaders - #4, #10, #16
Round - #3
Liner - 10/0

Tools & Other Supplies:
White latex paint or primer
Tracing paper & pencil
Transfer paper & stylus
Ruler
Matte spray sealer

INSTRUCTIONS

Preparation:
See pattern on page 38.
1. Prepare table for painting according to instructions in the "Furniture Preparation" section.
2. Apply a coat of white paint or primer to the entire table. Let dry.
3. Trace pattern of design from book onto tracing paper. Enlarge as needed to fit your table.
4. Transfer design to tabletop.

Painting the Design:
1. Basecoat inner rectangle with lavender.
2. Paint border and edges with heather. Paint dots with white.
3. Paint bee skep with clay bisque and butter pecan. Paint hole with black.
4. Paint bees' bodies with lemon. Paint wings with white. Paint stripes on bodies and heads with black.
5. Paint flower stems and leaves with pastel green. Paint flower petals with rose pink. Paint centers with lemon.
6. Paint base of bee skep with French blue. Paint stripes with peach.
7. Paint outlines and details with thinned black.

Painting the Trim:
1. Paint table apron with French blue. Let dry.
2. Draw checks with a ruler and pencil.
3. Paint checks with light blue. Add lines with thinned black.
4. Paint trim below apron with rose pink.
5. Paint shelf with French blue. Paint stripes on edges with peach. Add lines with black.
6. Paint tops of legs with lemon.
7. Paint middle section of legs with lavender. Paint dots with white. Add details with thinned black.
8. Paint bands above and below middle section with heather.
9. Paint bottoms of legs with rose pink. Let dry.

Finishing:
Spray with several coats of matte sealer. ❏

FOLK ART ANGEL TABLE

Created by Susan Fouts-Kline

This folk art angel is painted on a crackled background. The checkerboard design on the legs extends the country feeling.

SUPPLIES

Furniture Piece:
Square wooden end table with curved
 legs, 10" x 10"

Acrylic Craft Paint:
Almond parfait
Barn wood
Black
Brown mustard
Butter pecan
Clay bisque
Coffee bean
Huckleberry
Nutmeg
Southern pine
White

Artist's Paint Brushes:
Wash - 1"
Shader - #12
Round - #3
Liner - 10/0

Tools & Other Supplies:
White latex paint or primer
Crackle medium
Matte sealer spray
Tracing paper & pencil
Transfer paper & stylus

INSTRUCTIONS

Preparation & Crackling:
See pattern on page 39.
1. Prepare table for painting according to instructions in the "Furniture Preparation" section.
2. Apply a coat of white paint or primer to the entire table. Let dry.
3. Paint tabletop with clay bisque. Let dry.
4. Apply a thick coat of crackle medium. Let dry completely.
5. Brush tabletop with white. Cracks will form. Let dry.
6. Trace pattern from book onto tracing paper. Enlarge design as needed to fit your table.
7. Transfer design to tabletop.

Painting the Design:
1. Paint the wings with butter pecan.
2. Basecoat the face, hands, and legs with almond parfait.
3. Wash cheeks with Huckleberry.
4. Paint eyes, nose, and mouth with thinned black.
5. Basecoat dress with a mixture of three parts white and one part clay bisque.
6. Paint dots on dress with barn wood.
7. Paint shoes with clay bisque.
8. Shade with coffee bean.
9. Paint hair with layers of coffee bean, then highlight with brown mustard.
10. Paint grapevine garland with coffee bean. Paint leaves with southern pine. Paint berries with huckleberry.
11. Paint outlines, details, and halo with thinned black.

Painting the Trim Areas:
1. Paint outer edge of tabletop with clay bisque.
2. Paint leg stretchers with white.
3. Paint sides and insides of legs with clay bisque.
4. Paint outsides of legs with butter pecan. Paint checks with white. Let dry.

Finishing:
Spray with several coats matte sealer. ❏

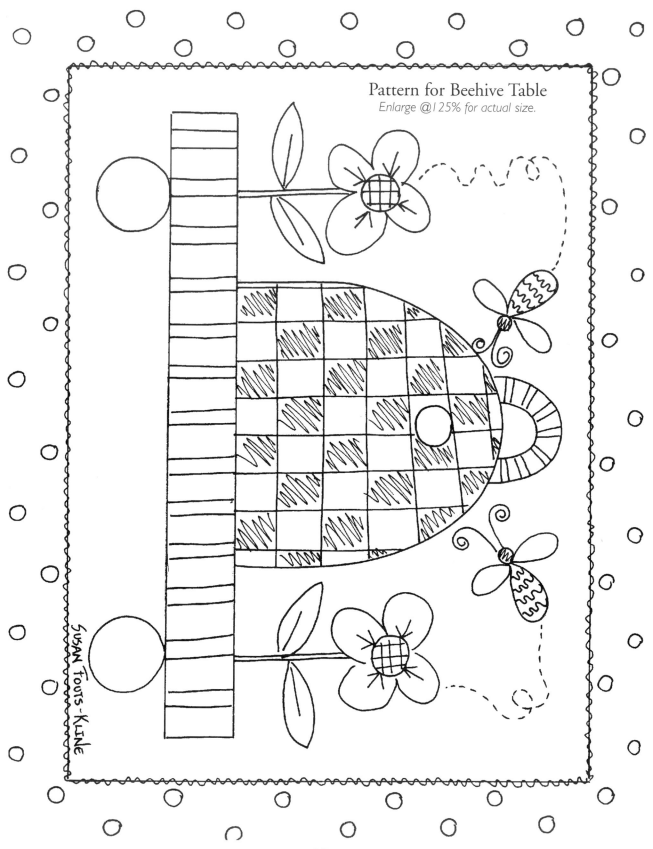

Pattern for Beehive Table
Enlarge @125% for actual size.

Susan Fouts-Kline

Pattern for Folk Art Angel Table
Actual Size Pattern

DRAGONFLY STOOL

Created by Holly Buttimer

*A painted dragonfly occupies center stage on this painted bar stool. The long legs
have a textured combed finish, and the colors are fresh and lively.*

SUPPLIES

Furniture Piece:
Wooden bar stool

Acrylic Paint:
Aqua
Black
Blue metallic
Bright pink
Bright yellow
Dark green
Dark brown
Gold metallic
Golden yellow
Green
Heather
Leaf green
Lemon yellow
Limelight
Orange
Purple
Red
Regency blue
Warm brown
White

Tools & Other Supplies:
Artist's paint brushes
Tracing paper & pencil
Transfer paper & stylus
Paint comb
Fine tip permanent marker
Matte spray sealer

INSTRUCTIONS

Preparation & Base Painting:
See patterns on pages 42, 43.
1. Prepare stool for painting according to the instructions in the "Furniture Preparation" section.
2. Paint the top with regency blue. Let dry.
3. Trace patterns from book onto tracing paper. Enlarge as needed to fit your stool.
4. Transfer design to the stool, using photo as a guide for placement.

Painting the Design:
Bee: Paint body with black and gold. Shade with yellow ochre. Highlight with lemonade. Paint wings with bright yellow. Shade wings with blue metallic.
Leaves: Paint with green. Shade at centers with dark green. Highlight with aqua and limelight.
Daisies: Paint petals with white. Shade with dark green. Paint centers with golden yellow. Shade with warm brown.
Dragonfly: Paint body with leaf green. Highlight with limelight, red, bright yellow, and bright pink. Shade with purple. Paint wings with streaks of leaf green, bright yellow, orange, bright pink, and purple.
Ladybug: Paint body with red and black. Shade with dark brown. Highlight with white and gold metallic.
Details: Add outlines and details with black paint, using a liner brush. For fine details, use a black fine tip permanent marker. Let dry.

Painting the Legs & Trim:
1. Paint squiggly line around design, stringers, and edge of top with heather. Let dry.
2. Paint dots on top and stringers with lemon yellow.
3. Paint legs with limelight. Let dry.
4. Working one leg at a time, brush legs with dark green. While paint is still wet, pull comb through paint to create wavy lines. Let dry.

Finishing:
Spray with matte sealer. Let dry. ❏

Pattern for Dragonfly Stool
Actual Size Pattern

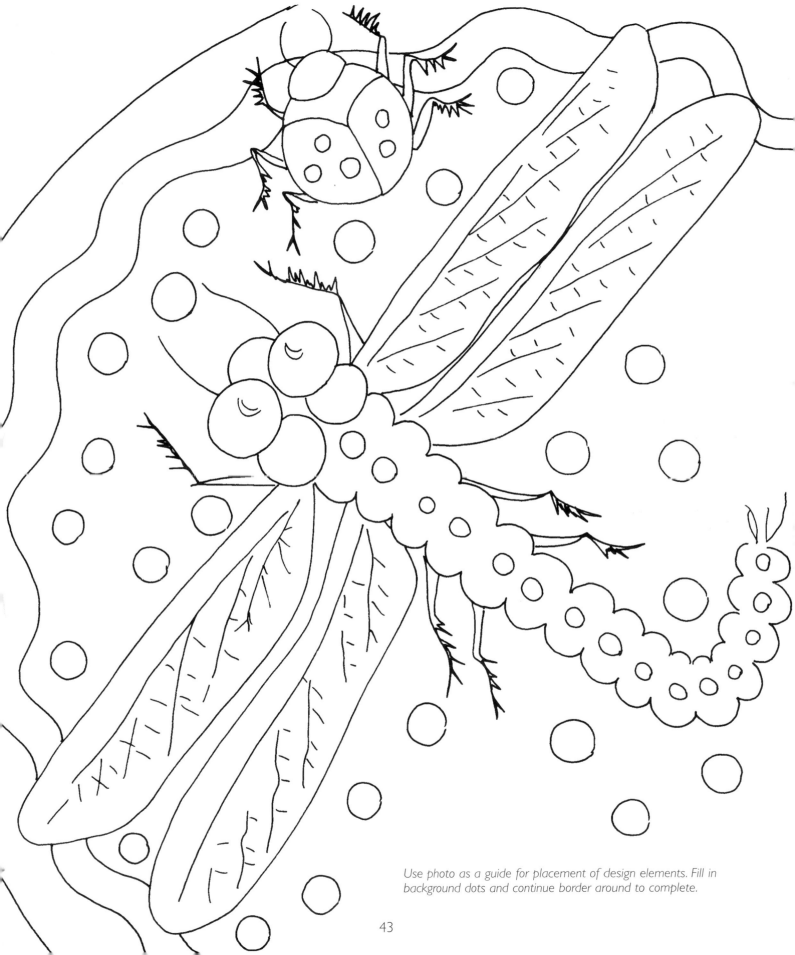

Use photo as a guide for placement of design elements. Fill in background dots and continue border around to complete.

43

DRAGONFLY BOWL

Created by Holly Buttimer

Fruit and flowers adorn this bowl, along with the dragonfly, butterflies, and ladybug. The same blue used on the top of the Dragonfly Bar Stool was used for the background on the inside of this bowl. The combed technique used on the bar stool legs decorates the outside of the bowl. Create an entire kitchen décor by painting variations of these design elements on stools, decorative bowls, plaques, or other areas of your kitchen.

SUPPLIES

Furniture Piece:
Shallow wooden bowl

Acrylic Paint:
Black
Blue metallic
Bright pink
Bright yellow
Copper metallic
Dark brown
Gold metallic
Lavender
Leaf green
Lemon yellow
Limelight
Olive
Orange
Purple
Red
Regency blue
Warm brown
White
Wild iris
Wine
Yellow ochre

Tools & Other Supplies:
Artist's paint brushes
Tracing paper & pencil
Transfer paper & stylus
Fine tip permanent marker
Comb
Matte spray sealer
Waterbase varnish

INSTRUCTIONS

Preparation:
See patterns on pages 46, 47.
1. Prepare wooden surface according to the instructions in the "Furniture Preparation" section.
2. Paint the inside of the bowl with regency blue. Let dry.
3. Trace patterns from book onto tracing paper. Enlarge or reduce as needed to fit your bowl.
4. Transfer designs to the bowl, using photo as a guide for placement.

Painting the Designs Inside:
Leaves: Paint with leaf green. Shade with olive. Highlight with limelight.
Pear: Paint with bright yellow. Paint spots and stem with warm brown. Shade with olive. Highlight with lemon yellow and copper metallic.
Ladybug: Paint body with red and black. Shade with dark brown. Highlight with white and gold metallic.
Pansies: Paint petals with lavender, wild iris, and purple. Highlight with white. Paint centers with orange, olive, and bright yellow.
Bee: Paint body with black and bright yellow. Shade with yellow ochre. Highlight with lemon yellow. Paint wings with bright yellow. Shade wings with blue metallic.
Dragonfly: Paint body with leaf green. Highlight with limelight, red, bright yellow, and bright pink. Shade with purple. Paint wings with streaks of leaf green, bright yellow, orange, pink, and purple.
Lemon: Paint with bright yellow. Shade with yellow ochre and copper metallic. Highlight with gold metallic and lemon yellow.
Apple: Paint with red. Shade with wine and dark brown. Highlight with orange and bright yellow.
Purple Butterfly Wings: Paint with lavender, wild iris, and dark purple. Highlight with white and bright yellow.
Orange Butterfly Wings: Paint wings with orange, yellow, white, and copper metallic. Shade with dark brown. Highlight with lemon yellow and white.
Butterfly Bodies: Paint bodies and antennae with black.
Details: Add outlines and details with black paint, using a liner brush. For fine details, use a black fine tip permanent marker. Let dry.

Continued on page 46

Patterns for Dragonfly Bowl
Enlarge @110% for actual size

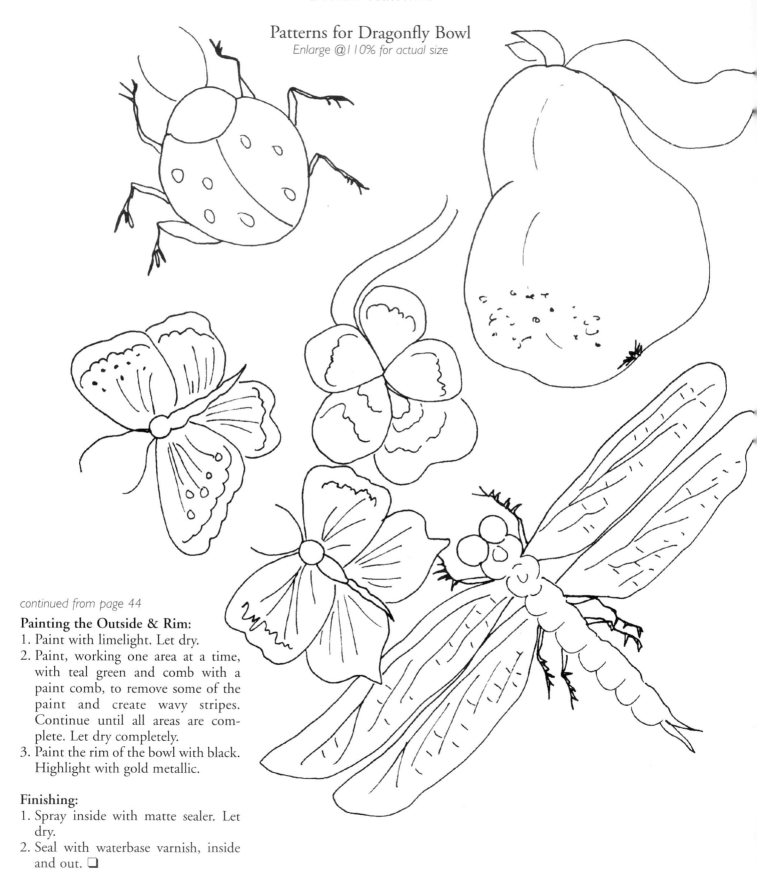

continued from page 44

Painting the Outside & Rim:
1. Paint with limelight. Let dry.
2. Paint, working one area at a time, with teal green and comb with a paint comb, to remove some of the paint and create wavy stripes. Continue until all areas are complete. Let dry completely.
3. Paint the rim of the bowl with black. Highlight with gold metallic.

Finishing:
1. Spray inside with matte sealer. Let dry.
2. Seal with waterbase varnish, inside and out. ❑

Use photo as a guide for placement of the design elements.

DRAGONFLY FRENCH BUCKET

Created by Holly Buttimer

Repeating the same motifs on accessories creates a coordinated, harmonious look. Varying the placement of motifs, colors, and backgrounds keeps things from getting monotonous and the effect is more sophisticated. The crackled background adds texture and surprise to this metal bucket.

SUPPLIES

Furniture Piece:
Tall metal French bucket

Acrylic Craft Paint:
Black
Blue metallic
Bright pink
Bright yellow
Copper metallic
Dark brown
Gold metallic
Lavender
Leaf green
Lemon yellow
Limelight
Olive
Orange
Purple
Red
Regency blue
White
Wild iris
Yellow ochre

Tools & Other Supplies:
Crackle medium
Artist's paint brushes
Tracing paper & pencil
Transfer paper & stylus
Fine tip permanent marker
Matte sealer spray
Waterbase varnish
Either: Sandpaper, 220 grit & tack
    cloth *or* vinegar & sponge

INSTRUCTIONS

Preparation
See patterns on pages 50, 51.
1. **If you're using a bucket with a galvanized finish,** wipe bucket inside and out with vinegar. Rinse. Let dry completely. **If your bucket has a painted finish,** sand surface with sandpaper. Wipe away dust.
2. Base paint bucket with black. Let dry.
3. Apply crackle medium. Let dry.
4. Paint bucket with regency blue. Cracks will form. Let dry.
5. Trace patterns from book onto tracing paper. Enlarge as needed to fit your bucket.
6. Transfer designs to bucket.

Painting the Design:
Butterfly: Paint with black. Highlight with bright pink, yellow ochre, lemon yellow, lavender, and white.
Dragonfly: Paint body with leaf green. Highlight with limelight, bright pink, blue metallic, purple, and gold metallic. Paint wings with white. Highlight with bright pink, regency blue, and limelight.
Ladybug: Paint body with red and black. Shade with dark brown. Highlight with white and gold metallic.
Pansies: Paint petals with lavender, wild iris, and purple. Highlight with white. Paint centers with orange, olive, and bright yellow.
Details: Add outlines and details with black paint, using a liner brush. For fine details, use a black fine tip permanent marker. Let dry.

Finishing:
1. Spray with matte sealer. Let dry.
2. Seal with waterbase varnish, inside and out. ❑

Pattern for Dragonfly Bucket
Actual Size Pattern

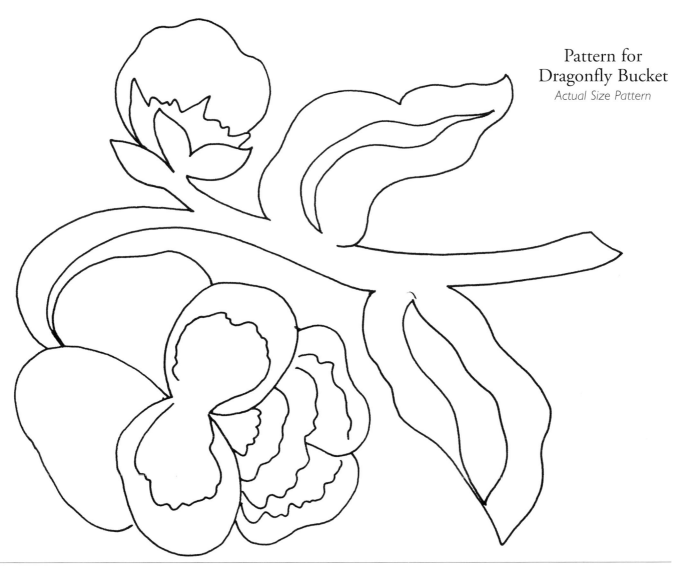

Painting Diagram

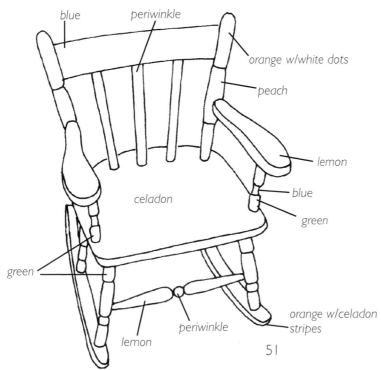

blue

periwinkle

orange w/white dots

peach

lemon

blue

green

celadon

green

orange w/celadon stripes

periwinkle

lemon

Bee Sweet Rocking Chair
See instructions on page 52

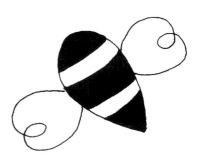

Pattern for Bee

BEE SWEET ROCKING CHAIR

Created by Lindsey Mahaffey

Children love having their names on their furniture; on this rocker, the child's name is spelled out in the broken lines of bees' flight trail. Wooden half-eggs are painted like bees' bodies and glued to the back of the chair to provide dimension and interest.

SUPPLIES

Furniture Piece:
Child's wooden rocking chair

Acrylic Craft Paint:
Black
Blue
Celadon
Green
Lemon
Orange
Peach
Periwinkle
White

Tools & Other Supplies:
Flat paint brushes
Small round brush
Cotton swabs
2 wooden half eggs, 7/8"
Wood glue
Tracing paper & pencil
Transfer paper & stylus
Waterbase varnish

INSTRUCTIONS

Preparation:
See pattern on page 51.
1. Prepare rocker for painting, following the instructions in the "Furniture Preparation" section.
2. Prime the half eggs with white paint.
3. Trace pattern for bee onto tracing paper.

Base Painting:
1. Paint the parts of the chair, using various flat brushes and the diagram on page 51 as a guide, with these colors:
    Seat - celadon
    Back - blue
    Side back pieces, top to bottom -
        orange, peach, celadon, orange
    Rockers - orange
    Arm rests - lemon
    Back supports - periwinkle
    Arm supports - green, blue, green
    Legs - green, celadon, blue, green
2. Let dry.

Design & Trim Painting:
1. Use a 1/2" flat brush to paint stripes on the rockers.
2. Dip a cotton swab in white paint and press on the top of the side back pieces to create dots. Vary pressure on the swab to vary the size of the dots.
3. Use a pencil to lightly write the child's name on the back of the rocker. Transfer the bee design to the seat and draw flight lines lightly on seat, using photo as a guide.
4. With the point of a small round brush, paint the name and flight lines with broken lines of black paint.

5. Paint the half eggs and the bee on the seat with lemon paint. Let dry.
6. Paint stripes on the bees with black, using a small round brush.
7. Glue wood pieces to back of rocker. Let dry.
8. Paint bees' wings with black paint. Let dry.

Finishing:
Apply several coats waterbase varnish. Let dry between coats. ❑

COLOR CHART

Celadon   *Lemon*   *Blue*   *Periwinkle*

Orange   *Peach*   *Green*

COUNTRY CHICKEN CHAIR

Created by Susan Fouts-Kline

Farm motifs – chickens, sunflowers, and a basket of apples – decorate this brightly colored chair. The same motifs could be used to create a coordinating cupboard or chest or to create a wall border.

SUPPLIES

Furniture Piece:
Wooden chair

Acrylic Craft Paint:
Fuchsia
Blue
Red
Orange
Kelly green
White
Black
Yellow
Violet
Green
Butter pecan
Coffee bean
Light red
Raw sienna
Pure orange

Artist's Paint Brushes:
Wash - 1"
Shaders - #4, #10, #16
Rounds - #3, #5
Liner - #10/0

Tools & Other Supplies:
Tracing paper & pencil
Transfer paper & stylus
Matte spray sealer

INSTRUCTIONS

Preparation:
See patterns on pages 56, 57.
1. Prepare chair for paint, following instructions in the "Furniture Preparation" section.
2. Base paint chair seat with two coats blue. Paint center back piece of chair with two coats red. Paint top of chair back with two coats light red. Let dry between coats.
3. Trace patterns from book onto tracing paper. Enlarge as needed to fit your chair.
4. Transfer designs to chair, using photo as a guide for placement.

Painting the Designs:
Hen on Chair Seat:
1. Paint hen's beak and legs with orange.
2. Paint wattle and comb with red.
3. Paint body with black. Paint dots with violet.
4. Undercoat eye with white. Paint with yellow. Paint center with black.
5. Paint cherries with red. Highlight with comma strokes of white. Paint stems with coffee bean.
6. Paint leaves with kelly green. Add veins with green.
7. Paint basket with raw sienna. Paint trim with butter pecan.
8. Undercoat chick's body with white. Paint with yellow. Paint beak and legs with orange. Paint wing with violet. Paint eye with black.
9. Outline with thinned black.

Center Back:
1. Paint stems and leaves with kelly green. Paint leaf veins with green.
2. Undercoat flower petals and centers with white.
3. Paint petals with yellow. Paint centers with pure orange. Add dots with black.
4. Paint outlines and details with thinned black.

Top of Back:
1. Undercoat chicks with white. Paint with yellow.
2. Paint beaks and legs with orange. Paint wing with violet. Paint eye with black.
3. Paint cherry with red. Highlight with a comma stroke of white. Paint stem with coffee bean.
4. Paint leaf with kelly green. Add vein with green.
5. Outline with thinned black.

Painting the Trim:
1. Paint side pieces of chair back with fuchsia.

Continued on page 56

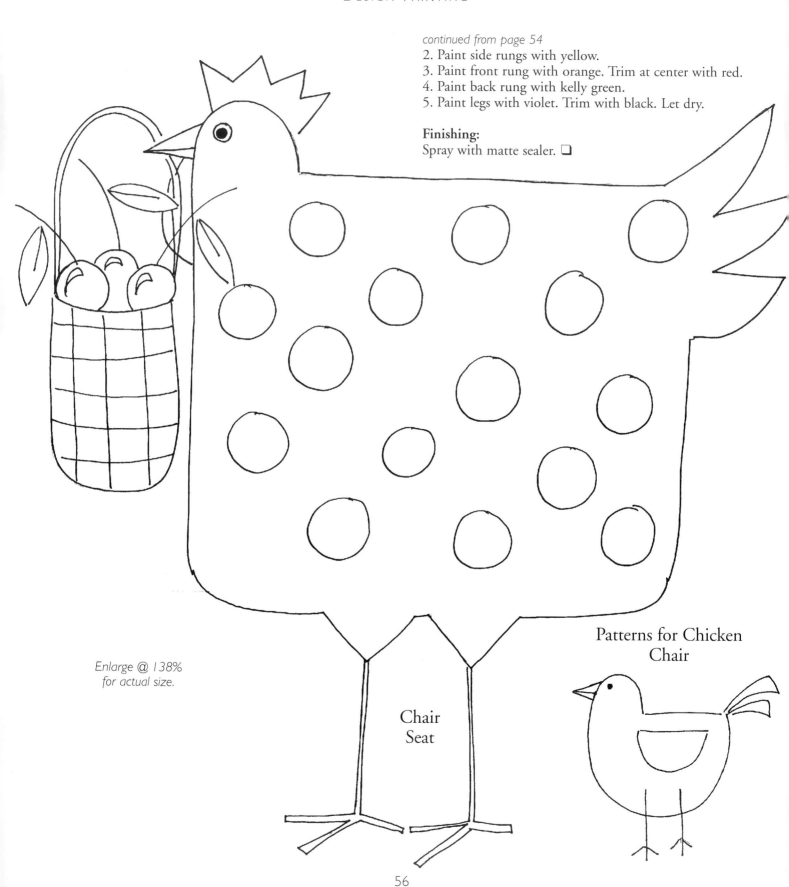

continued from page 54
2. Paint side rungs with yellow.
3. Paint front rung with orange. Trim at center with red.
4. Paint back rung with kelly green.
5. Paint legs with violet. Trim with black. Let dry.

Finishing:
Spray with matte sealer. ❑

*Enlarge @ 138%
for actual size.*

Chair
Seat

Patterns for Chicken
Chair

Center Back

Top Back

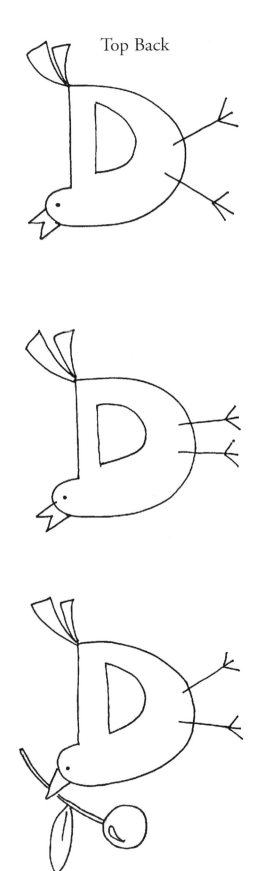

*Enlarge @ 138%
for actual size.*

FLOWER GARDEN TABLE

Created by Susan Fouts-Kline

This simple pine table becomes something special with the addition of painted designs on the top and the legs. The table was stained, rather than painted, creating a warm wood-toned background for the garden-themed motifs.

SUPPLIES

Furniture Piece:
Stained square end wooden table,
　10-1/2" square

Acrylic Craft Paint:
Aspen green
Autumn leaves
Black
Clay bisque
Coffee bean
Green forest
Heartland blue
Hunter green
Honeycomb
Huckleberry
Linen
Purple
Settler's blue
Turner's yellow
White

Artist's Paint Brushes:
Rounds - #4
Liner - 10/0
Shaders - #4, #8, #14

Tools & Other Supplies:
Matte sealer spray
Tracing paper & pencil
Transfer paper & stylus

INSTRUCTIONS

Preparation:
See patterns on pages 60, 61.
1. Trace patterns from book onto tracing paper. Enlarge as needed to fit your table.
2. Transfer designs to tabletop and legs.

Painting the Designs:
Floral Design on Tabletop:
　1. Basecoat circle with clay bisque.
　2. Paint leaves with aspen green, hunter green, and green forest, using photo as a guide for placement.
　3. Paint the blue petaled flowers with settler's blue. Base centers with heartland blue. Paint circles inside centers with Turner's yellow. Add white dots.
　4. Paint round flowers with Turner's yellow. Paint centers with autumn leaves. Add hatch marks in centers with black. Add comma stroke highlights with white.
　5. Paint large flower's petals with huckleberry. Paint the center circle with honeycomb. Paint the flower design inside the circle with black. add a white dot.
　6. Paint the berries with purple. Add comma stroke highlights with white.
　7. Paint tendrils with aspen green.
　8. Paint clusters of dots with black.
　9. Add dots around design with huckleberry, using photo as a guide for placement.
10. Paint outlines and details with thinned black.
11. Shade painted designs with coffee bean, using photo as a guide. Let dry.

Bees on Table Legs:
1. Paint bodies with Turner's yellow. Paint wings with linen.
2. Paint heads and stripes with black.
3. Paint outlines and details with thinned black.

Painting the Trim:
1. Paint outer band around circle and the edge of the lower shelf with white. Add stripes with black.
2. Paint inner band around circle and edges of tabletop with heartland blue.

Finishing:
Spray table with several coats of matte sealer. ❑

Patterns for Flower Garden Table
Actual Size Patterns

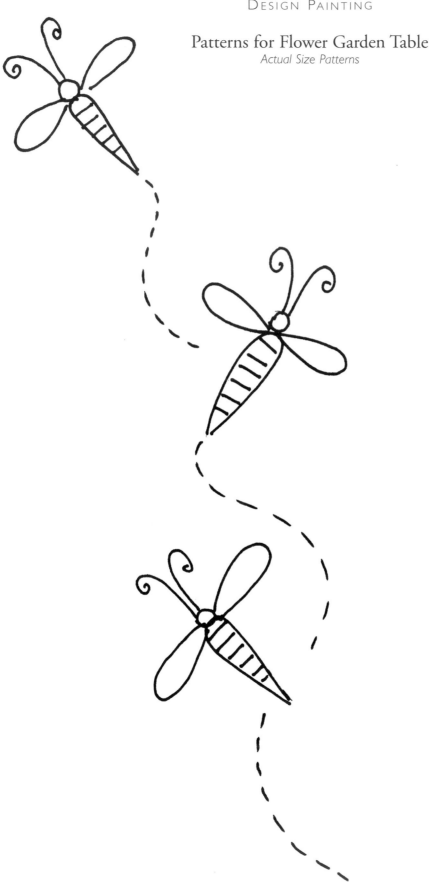

*Connect pattern
at dotted line*

BLACK & WHITE BAR STOOL

Created by Kirsten Jones

After painting and sanding, the entire surface of this bar stool received an application of wood-tone stain that subdues and unifies the colors. The distressed finish gives an Old World look to the rose and leaf motifs.

SUPPLIES

Furniture Piece:
Wooden bar stool with back

Acrylic Paint:
Black
White
Basil green
Sunflower yellow
Burgundy

Paint Brushes:
Rounds - #8, #4
Flat - 1"

Tools & Other Supplies:
Sandpaper
Wax stick
Wood stain - walnut
Tracing paper
Transfer paper
Gloss spray sealer

INSTRUCTIONS

Preparation:
1. Prepare wood surface according to instructions in the "Furniture Preparation" section.
2. Rub wax stick on edges of chair and randomly on other areas of chair.

Creating a Distressed Painted Finish:
1. Paint different sections of chair with different colors, using photo as a guide for placement. Let dry.
2. Sand chair to create a distressed finish. Where wax was applied, paint will readily come off.
3. Stain chair, rubbing stain into areas where paint was removed. Let dry.

Painting the Design:
See patterns on page 65.
1. Trace patterns from book onto tracing paper and enlarge as needed.
2. Transfer design to seat of chair, repeating design to cover entire seat.
3. Paint pattern on seat, using #8 brush with white paint.
4. Transfer rose design to back of chair.
5. Paint rose design, using basil green for leaves and vine and sunflower yellow for roses. Let dry.
6. Outline design with black, using a #4 brush. Let dry completely.

Finishing:
Spray chair with gloss sealer. ❏

Pictured above: Closeup view of seat detail on Bar Stool

Pattern for Bar Stool
Actual Size Pattern

Chair Seat

Chair Back
*Reverse vine and repeat
on opposite side.*

ROUND PARLOR TABLE

Created by Lindsey Mahaffey

This painted design, on the tabletop only, is a great way to refurbish a table that has a damaged top. The tone on tone design is easy to paint, and because you're only working on the top and leaving the base alone, it's a really quick fix.

SUPPLIES

Furniture Piece:
Round pedestal table

Acrylic Paint:
Black
Brick
Burnt sienna
Terra cotta

Tools & Other Supplies:
Tracing paper & pencil
Transfer paper & stylus
Flat paint brushes, 1", 2"
Waterbase varnish

INSTRUCTIONS

Preparation:
See pattern on page 126.
1. Prepare tabletop for painting, following instructions in the "Furniture Preparation" section and leaving the pedestal base in its original stained condition.
2. Paint only the tabletop with a brick color, using a 2" flat brush. Let dry.
3. Use a 1" flat brush to paint the rim of the tabletop with burnt sienna.
4. Trace the pattern for the border. Enlarge on a copy machine. Transfer to the edge of the table.

Painting the Designs:
1. Use a 1/4" round brush to paint the design on the edge of the table with black. Let dry.

COLOR CHART

Burnt sienna   Brick   Terra cotta   Black

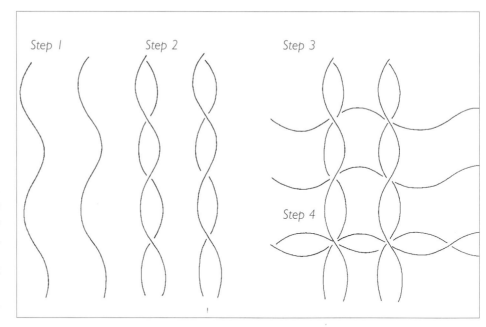

Step 1   Step 2   Step 3

Step 4

2. Using a liner brush, paint the woven design freehand with terra cotta in four steps, as shown above. Let dry.

Finishing:
Apply several coats of waterbase varnish to the tabletop. Let dry between coats. ❏

CHEETAH TABLE

Created by Holly Buttimer

Leopard spots and zebra and tiger stripes decorate the legs and border of this jungle-themed table with a cheetah's face at the center of the top. Metallic accents add shine and sparkle.

SUPPLIES

Furniture Piece:
Round wooden table, 24" diameter

Acrylic Paint:
Black
Copper metallic
Dark brown
Gold metallic
Medium brown
Pale yellow
Tan
White
Yellow ochre

Tools & Other Supplies:
Sponge brushes
Artist's paint brushes - flats and rounds
Sea sponge
Masking tape
Tracing paper & pencil
Transfer paper & stylus
Acrylic varnish

INSTRUCTIONS

Preparation:
See patterns on pages 70, 71.
1. Prepare table for painting according to instructions in the "Furniture Preparation" section.
2. Trace pattern from book onto tracing paper. Enlarge as needed to fit your table.
3. Transfer design to table.

Painting the Tabletop:
Cheetah:
1. Paint center circle with black.
2. Paint border with gold metallic. Outline with black.

COLOR CHART

Gold metallic   Tan   Copper metallic   Black

Dark brown   Pale yellow   Yellow ochre   White   Medium brown

3. Paint cheetah's fur with tan, yellow ochre, white, and black.
4. Highlight with copper metallic and gold metallic.
5. Paint eyes with yellow ochre. Highlight with gold metallic. Paint pupils with black. Outline eyes with black. Add white dots to highlight. Paint lashes with black.
6. Paint nose with black. Highlight with white.
7. Shade cheetah and gold border with dark brown.

Areas with Leopard Spots:
1. Basecoat with tan. Let dry.
2. Paint spots with medium brown.
3. Highlight with gold metallic and copper metallic.
4. Outline with black.

Zebra-Striped Insets:
1. Basecoat with white.
2. Paint stripes with black.

Tiger-Striped Edge:
1. Basecoat with gold metallic. Let dry.
2. Sponge with copper metallic. Let dry.
3. Paint stripes with black.

Painting the Legs:
1. Paint legs with various animal skin patterns, using the colors above.
2. Paint bands of trim with gold metallic and copper metallic.
3. Paint feet with gold metallic. let dry. Sponge with copper metallic. Let dry.

Finishing:
Apply two to three coats of varnish to seal. ❏

Pattern for Cheetah Table
Actual Size Patterns

Spots for
background

Stripes for
border

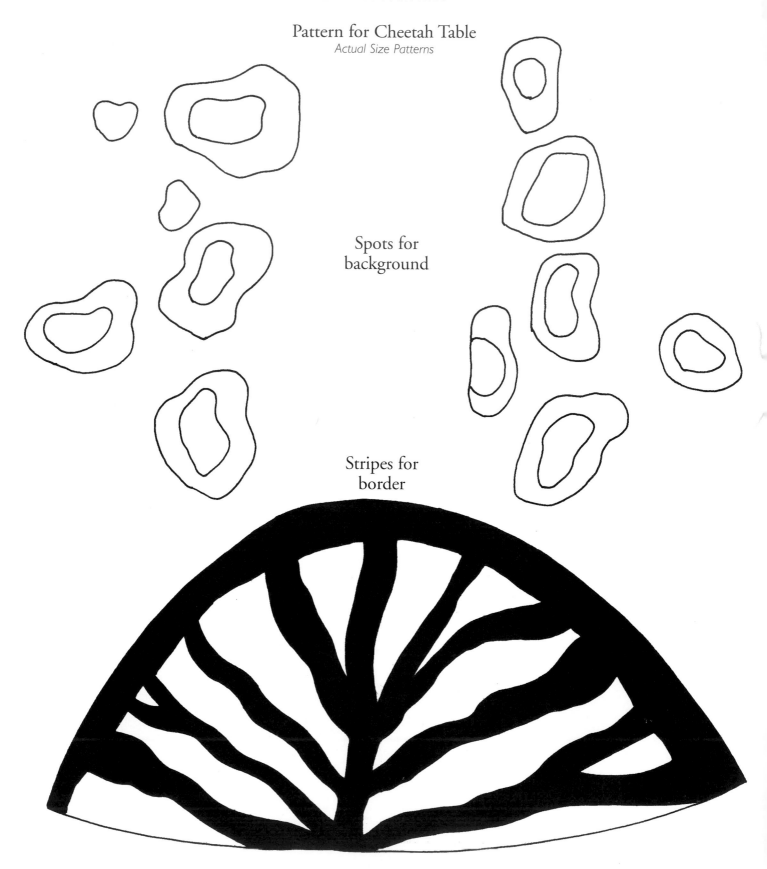

Center of Table

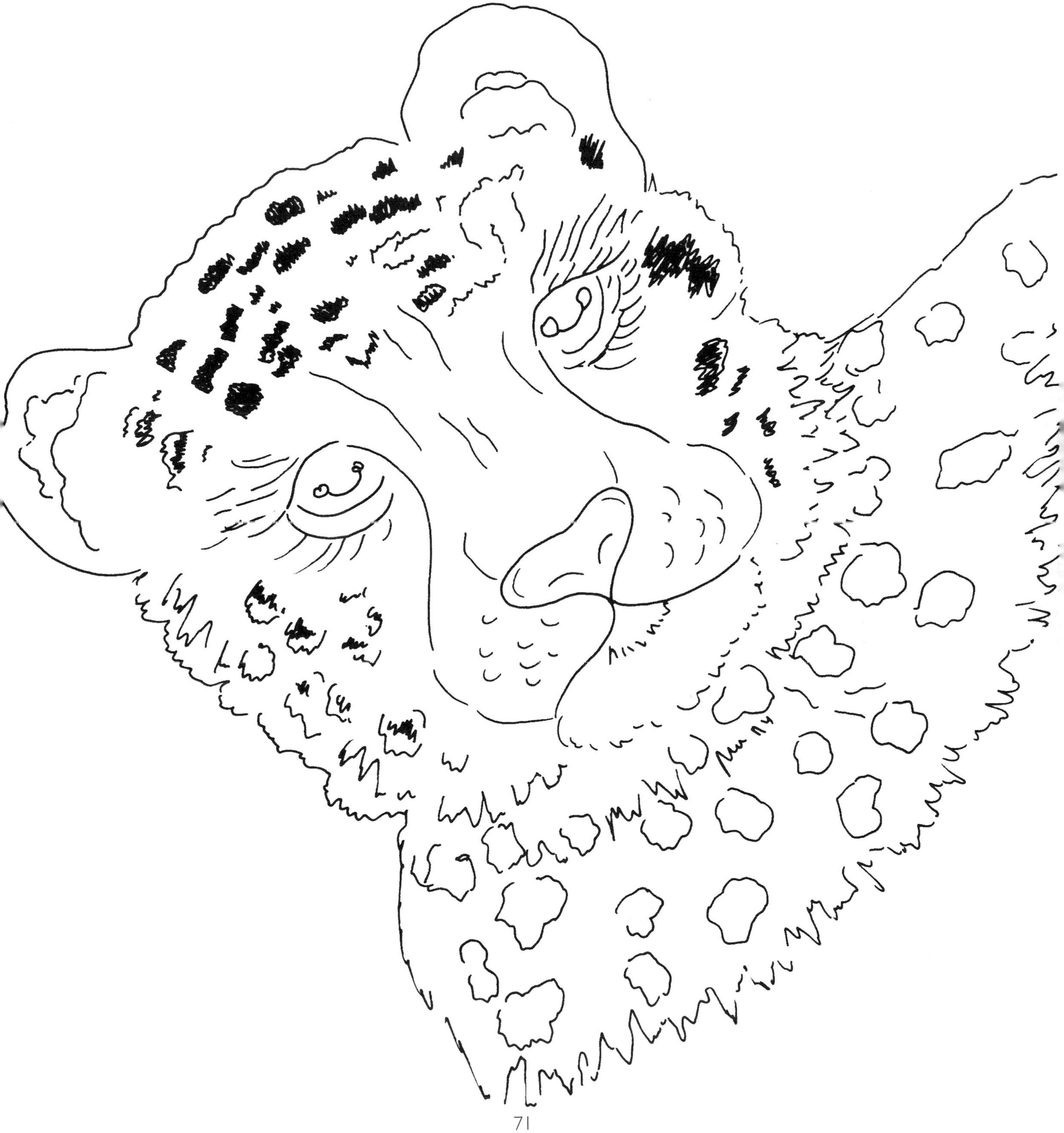

Distressing

Distressed finishes add the character imparted by use and age. You can create a simple distressed finish by painting a piece with layers of color and sanding after the paint has dried. This removes some of the paint, exposing layers of color and allowing some of the wood to show. Applying wax to the surface between layers of paint makes the succeeding coats easier to remove.

BASIC SUPPLIES

- Acrylic paint, two (or more) colors
- Sandpaper - medium, medium-fine, and fine
- Wax stick, to apply to surface to make paint easier to remove
- Metal scraper
- Foam brush, for base painting
- Tack cloth

HERE'S HOW

1. Paint piece with first paint color. (**photo 1**) Let dry.
2. Apply wax to areas of piece where wear would normally occur. (**photo 2**) This will allow top later of paint to sand off and separate from the bottom layer.
3. Paint with second paint color. (**photo 3**) Let dry.
4. Sand and/or scrape paint to reveal paint layers and/or bare wood. (**photo 4**)
5. After sanding, use a tack cloth to wipe away dust. ❑

Sanding Tips

- Sand more on the edges of the piece – concentrating your efforts in places where wear would normally occur over time – and less on flat areas for a more natural appearance.

- Don't use a sanding block or an electric sander – you want an uneven look. Holding the sandpaper in your hand is best and allows you more control.

- Use medium or medium-fine grit sandpaper to remove more paint, fine grit sandpaper to remove less.

- It's best to begin slowly and err on the side of removing too little paint rather than too much. You can always sand again to remove more. Stop when the result pleases you.

Photo 1. Paint first color.

Photo 2. Apply wax.

Photo 3. Paint second color.

Photo 4. Sand.

DISTRESSED CHEST OF DRAWERS

Created by Kathi Bailey

Kathi Bailey changed the look of this chest of drawers (you can see her "Before" photo on page 76) by removing the corner hardware, adding wooden rope molding to the edges, and creating a really quick distressed finish with a taupe spray paint undercoat and a white latex topcoat.

SUPPLIES

Furniture Piece:
Wooden dresser

Paint:
White latex paint
Gold metallic spray paint
Taupe spray paint

Tools & Other Supplies:
Wax stick, to apply to surface to make paint easier to remove
Sandpaper - 100 grit, 220 grit
Wooden rope molding (enough to fit around edges and sides)
Handheld electric sander
Miter box and saw
Hammer
Wood glue
Finishing nails
Sponge brush
Tack cloth
Measuring tape & pencil
Acrylic spray sealer

Instructions follow on page 76.

Distressed Chest of Drawers (cont.)

INSTRUCTIONS

Preparation:
1. Remove drawer pulls and metal trim. Discard trim.
2. Spray drawer pulls with gold metallic paint. Let dry.
3. Lightly sand entire dresser to remove sheen. Wipe with a tack cloth.
4. Measure front edges and sides for molding. Saw moldings to fit, mitering corners.
5. Attach molding with nails and wood glue.

Painting:
1. Spray entire dresser with two light coats of taupe. Let dry.
2. Rub wax stick over areas where you want to distress. Rub over areas that would naturally get more wear.
3. Paint with two coats of white latex paint. Let dry two hours.

Distressing:
1. Sand dresser with 100 grit sandpaper to distress, emphasizing corners and other areas where wear would naturally occur. Sand down to bare wood in spots.
2. Finish with 220 grit sandpaper to smooth. Wipe with a tack cloth.

Finishing:
Apply two coats of spray sealer. Let dry between coats. ❑

Before painting

Fabric Fixes

Fabric is a wonderful way to change, cover up, renew, and coordinate furniture – it can be used for quick upholstered chair seats, quick coverups, slipcovers, and draped coverings.

When purchasing fabric, it is best to buy thin upholstery-grade fabric rather than dressmaker fabric. Upholstery fabric is stronger, and the fabric patterns and colors will be more suited to home decor.

Fabric shops specializing in home decorating fabrics can be found in most cities.

The color, design, texture, and sensuality of some fabrics are so tempting that I sometimes find it impossible to resist buying a piece for future use. Buying fabrics can be an addiction. I have boxes and boxes of beautiful fabrics stored away for those quilts or slipcovers that I am going to do "someday."

STAMPED VELVET CHAIR SEAT

The fabric for these chairs was stamped to create a custom-coordinated print that matches the stamping on the chair backs. See "Stamping" section (beginning on page 104) for complete instructions to create the chair seat and matching stamped chair.

MIX & MATCH DINING CHAIRS

Created by Mickey Baskett

When it came time to recover my dining room chairs, I was in big trouble. I fell in love with several fabrics and could not decide which to buy, so I asked my fabric-lover friend, Susan Mickey, to help me. Between the two of us we could not settle on just one fabric, so we chose four fabrics we loved that would work well together. Using four fabrics for my eight chairs resulted in a beautiful mix-and-match look. The trick to mixing and matching is to keep the fabrics all within the same color range and same types of fabric. The four fabrics we chose were silk upholstery-grade fabric. Recovering your own chair seats is very easy and quick and requires very few tools. Providing your chairs are in good condition, covering each chair takes only about an hour (or less).

SUPPLIES

Upholstery fabric (amount depends upon size of chair)
Optional: Blackout lining or muslin to cover bottom of chair seat
Ruler or measuring tape
Scissors
Heavy-duty staple gun
Screwdriver

Instructions follow on page 82.

Mix & Match Dining Chairs (cont.)

INSTRUCTIONS

Preparation:

1. Remove chair seat from chair. (This usually requires only a screwdriver.) (**photo 1**)
2. Measure chair seat to determine amount of fabric needed. Be sure to include the depth of the seat to arrive at the measurement. Add an extra 3" to each dimension to turn under and attach on the bottom. For most chair seats, you will be able to get two seats on the width of the fabric. Cut fabric to size needed.
3. Remove all old fabric from chair seat if it is in bad condition. If it is in good condition, leave it as extra padding.

Photo 1. Remove chair seat from chair.

Photo 2. Centering chair seat on fabric.

Upholstering:

1. Place fabric, right side down, on a clean work surface. Place chair seat, right side down, on top of fabric, centering chair seat on fabric. (**photo 2**)
2. Bring one side of fabric around to back side of seat. Fold fabric edge under and staple to seat at center of side length. (**photo 3**)
3. On the opposite side of the seat, pull fabric taut across seat to back of seat. Turn under edge and staple in place.
4. Repeat on the other two sides, pulling fabric taut each time. You will have stapled the fabric at the center of each side – this will keep the fabric tight and in place as you finish the sides.
5. Turn under and staple fabric in place along all four sides, stapling up to 2" from each corner. (**photo 4**)
6. At each corner, cut the fabric across the corner about 1-1/2" from end of corner. (This is called "mitering.") (**photo 5**)
7. Pull up fabric across corner and staple in place. At each side of corner, pull up fabric, fold under, and staple in place. (**photo 6**)

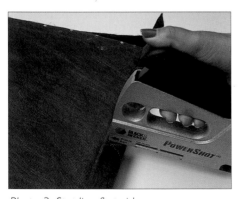

Photo 3. Stapling first side.

Photo 4. Stapling the fourth side.

Finishing:

1. *Optional:* If the bottom of your chair is unsightly, cut a piece of blackout lining to fit. Fold under edges and glue or staple in place.
2. Replace seat in chair. ❑

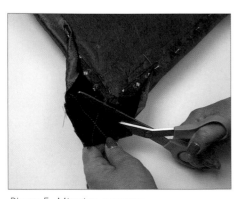

Photo 5. Mitering a corner.

Photo 6. Stapling a corner.

WRAPPED SLIPCOVERS FOR PATIO CHAIRS

Created by Susan Mickey

When your plastic or vinyl-coated patio dining chairs start to look old and stained, but they are otherwise still solid and usable, don't throw them away! Instead, slipcover them in bright, washable terrycloth towels. This quick coverup requires minimal sewing.

Instructions follow on page 86.

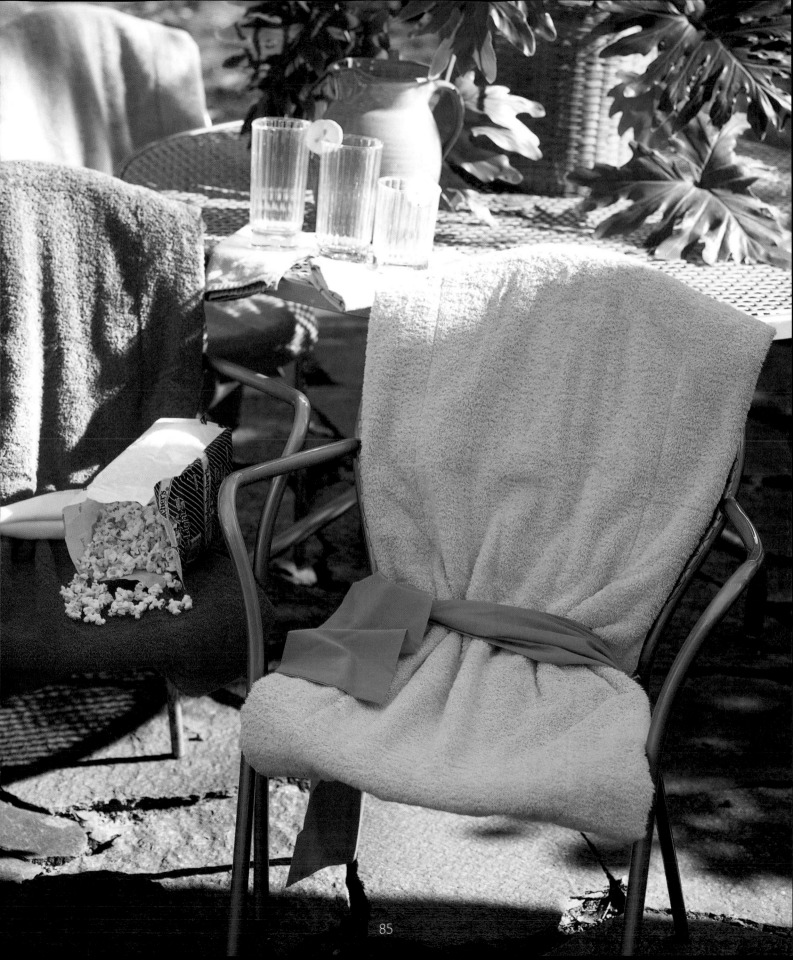

WRAPPED SLIPCOVERS FOR PATIO CHAIRS

Created by Susan Mickey

SUPPLIES

Furniture Piece:
Patio chair(s)

Fabric:
2 beach towels or terry bath sheets per chair, in complementary colors OR terrycloth fabric

1/2 yd. woven cotton broadcloth per chair, in contrasting colors for sash (OR wide grosgrain ribbon)

Tools & Other Supplies:
Thread to match
Hook-and-loop closure strips
Large, long-headed quilter's pins
Measuring tape
Iron and ironing board

INSTRUCTIONS

Measuring:
1. Measure height of seat back and depth of seat. See Fig. A.
2. To determine length of slipcover, add height and depth. Multiply by two. Add 6" for overlap. The towels sewn together end to end or the terrycloth fabric must be this length.

Sewing the Slipcover:
1. Sew the towels together end to end. Press seam open. Hem cut end(s).
2. Measure width of chair. Cut towels or fabric if needed. Hem long edges of towels or terrycloth fabric to achieve chair width.
3. Stitch pairs of hook-and-loop strips to both ends of slipcover.

Sewing the Sash:
1. Cut fabric crosswise (selvage to selvage) in 8" strips.
2. Sew short ends together to make a strip three times as long as the width of the fabric, less seam allowances. Press seams open.
3. Fold lengthwise and sew long sides together, leaving an opening for turning. Turn. Press, turning under raw edges of opening.
4. Slipstitch opening closed.
5. Edgestitch sash.

Fitting the Slipcover:
1. Wrap terrycloth slipcover around chair. (**photo 1**) This will form a loop that goes around the front and underside of chair.
2. Match hook-and-loop strips and press to secure. (**photo 2**)
3. Place sash around chair where seat meets back. Tie at back or on side. (**photo 3**) ❏

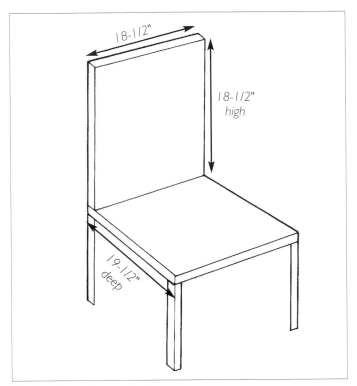

Fig. A - Measuring the chair.

Photo 1. Wrapping slipcover around chair.

Photo 2. Secure with hook and loop fastener.

Photo 3. Tie sash at back.

Glass Etching

Glass etching cream can be purchased at crafts and hardware stores. It's a terrific way to create a custom design on an otherwise plain tabletop. Stencils and masking tape are used to create the etched design. If the table will get lots of use, apply etching cream to underside of glass.

BASIC SUPPLIES

- Glass
- Glass etching cream
- Stencils and/or masking tape to create the design

HERE'S HOW

1. Clean glass.
2. Apply masking tape or affix stencil with stencil adhesive.
3. Apply etching cream, following manufacturer's instructions.
4. Wait recommended amount of time (usually about five minutes) and rinse. Remove tape or stencil.

GLASS TOPPED COFFEE TABLE

Created by Kathi Bailey

SUPPLIES

Furniture Piece:
Coffee table with glass top and
    metal base

Tools & Other Supplies:
Glass etching cream
Spray paint - black
Stencils with fern motifs
Spray stencil adhesive
Masking tape, 1"
Glass cleaner
Paper towels

INSTRUCTONS

Preparation:
1. Remove glass top from base.
2. Spray base with two coats black paint.
3. Clean glass top with glass cleaner. Wipe dry.

Etching:
1. Mask off a 1-1/2" border 1" from edge of tabletop. Mask off a 10" diamond in center.
2. Apply etching cream to border and center diamond, following manufacturer's instructions.
3. Wait recommended amount of time (usually about five minutes) and rinse. Remove tape.
4. Apply spray stencil adhesive to backs of fern stencils. Position, one at a time, in four quadrants of table, using photo as a guide. Apply etching cream to area inside stencil. Wait recommended amount of time. Rinse. Repeat in remaining quadrants.
5. Dry. Place tabletop in base. ❑

Gold Leafing

Glass etching cream can be purchased at crafts and hardware stores. It's a terrific way to create a custom design on an otherwise plain tabletop.
Gold leafing is an elegant, traditional way to add a warm metallic glow to surfaces. Leafing sheets and leaf adhesive are easy to use and available at art supply and crafts stores.

BASIC SUPPLIES

- Acrylic paint - dark red
- Gold metal leaf
- Leaf adhesive
- Pencil with eraser
- Foam brush
- Soft bristle brush, 3/4" or #12 flat

HERE'S HOW

1. Paint area to be leafed with dark red paint. Let dry. (**photo 1**)
2. Brush leaf adhesive over area and let dry, following manufacturer's instructions. (**photo 2**)
3. Apply sheets of leafing to cover adhesive, one sheet at a time. (**photo 3**) To pick up leafing sheets, use the eraser end of a pencil after moistening the eraser by touching it to a damp (not wet) cloth. Lightly press the leafing on the surface, using the soft brush. Repeat, overlapping each piece, until the surface is covered.
4. Pounce surface lightly with a soft brush to smooth. (**photo 4**) ❏

Photo 1. Painting area to be gold leafed with dark red acrylic paint.

Photo 2. Applying leaf adhesive to the surface.

Photo 3. Floating on a sheet of gold leaf.

Photo 4. Pouncing with a soft, flat brush to adhere leafing.

GOLD LEAFED PEDESTAL TABLE

Created by Kirsten Jones

*This elegant table is quick and easy to create. If your table is in good condition,
as this one was, no preparation is necessary, except to be sure the top is clean and dry.
As the top will be painted and covered, this is an ideal treatment for a table with
a damaged top.*

SUPPLIES

Furniture Piece:
Round-top pedestal table

Acrylic Paint:
Dark red

Tools & Other Supplies:
Gold metal leaf
Brush-on leaf adhesive
3/4" flat brush
Soft cloth
Matte spray sealer

INSTRUCTIONS

Apply Leafing:
1. Apply adhesive to top of table, following manufacturer's instructions. Let dry as recommended.
2. Apply gold leafing to top of table, overlapping each piece for a solid gold finish.
3. Rub off excess gold leaf with soft cloth.

Finishing:
Seal with light coat of matte sealer. If the tabletop is going to get lots of use, cover with a piece of glass to size, or several coats of polyurethane varnish. ❏

Solid Color Painting

Creating a painted design that consists of solid blocks of color is a great way to decorate a furniture piece. It's also a great way to create a furniture piece that can serve as a focal point in a room and pull together all the colors in the room for a custom, coordinated look. Sometimes referred to as "color block painting," solid color painting is as simple as coloring in a coloring book or painting by numbers – there's no shading or highlighting to do. With the wide range of pre-mixed colors available in acrylic craft paints, your color choices and combinations are practically limitless.

HARLEQUIN COFFEE TABLE

Created by Lindsey Mahaffey

Diamonds of color and black and white checks decorate this whimsical coffee table pictured on pages 96 and 97. Wooden wheels on the legs and turned finials at the corners, painted with the colors from the tabletop design, add dimension and interest. The colors and ideas from this design could be adapted to any table.

The dots can be painted with the tip of a small round brush, or you can use the eraser of a new pencil. Simply dip the eraser in a small amount of paint and "stamp" the eraser on the surface to make the dot.

SUPPLIES

Furniture Piece:
Wooden coffee table (This table is 32" x 24", and 18" tall.)

Acrylic Paint:

Black	Green	Mustard
Pink	Purple	Red
Teal	Turquoise	White

Tools & Other Supplies:
Paint brushes, flats and rounds in assorted sizes
Pencil & ruler

Tracing paper
Transfer paper & stylus
Masking tape
16 wooden wheels, 2" diameter
4 wooden finials, 1-7/8" square at base, 4-1/2" tall
16 nails to fit holes in wheels, 1-1/2" long
4 double-ended screws
Drill and drill bits to fit nails and screws
Hammer
Matte spray sealer

INSTRUCTIONS

Preparation:
1. Prepare the table and wooden pieces for painting according to the instructions in the "Furniture Preparation" section.

Continued on next page

Tips for Painting

- To get clean, crisp, straight lines, mask off alternating sections and paint. Remove tape. Let dry completely before taping over previously painted areas.
- Add decorative elements such as dots, stripes, and checks or simple designs such as vines and squiggles.
- Let the architecture of the furniture piece dictate the color breaks – choose tables with aprons, chairs with spindles and turned legs, etc.
- Consider adding architecture to your piece in the form of wooden cutouts – half eggs, half circles, finials, wheels. Paint in accenting or contrasting colors. Attach with glue, screws, or nails.

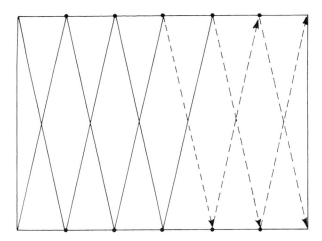

Fig. A - mark table top diamonds

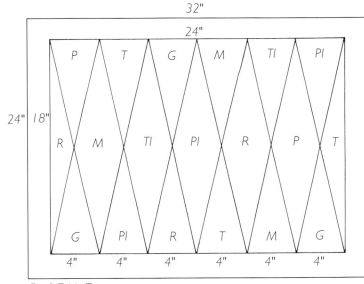

32"

24"

24" | 18"

P	T	G	M	TI	PI
R	M	TI	PI	R	P	T
G	PI	R	T	M	G

4" 4" 4" 4" 4" 4"

Fig. B Table Top

R - Red   G - Green   PI - Purple
P - Pink   T - Turquoise   TI - Teal
                                  M - Mustard

COLOR CHART

Red

Purple

Mustard

Pink

Turquoise

Teal

Green

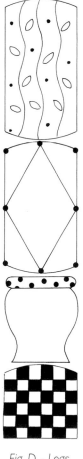

Fig. D - Legs

Fig. C - Mark diamonds on leg sections.

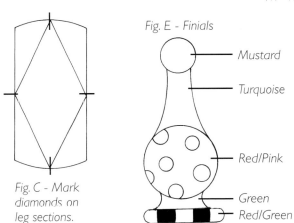

Fig. E - Finials

Mustard

Turquoise

Red/Pink

Green

Red/Green

2. With a pencil and ruler, draw a rectangle on the tabletop that measures 24" x 18". On each long side of the rectangle, measure and mark every 4". Connect pairs of lines with Xs to form a pattern of elongated diamonds and triangles. *See Fig. A.*

Painting the Table Top:
See Fig. B above and pattern on page 126.
1. Paint the area of the tabletop outside the rectangle, the table apron, and the corner pieces (top of leg) with black. Let dry.
2. To make the checks on the apron, use a 3/4" flat brush with white paint. (This size brush will make squares about 7/8".)
3. Trace the vine design and enlarge for the tabletop. Transfer to area around rectangle.
4. Using a small round brush, paint vines with green.

Continued on next page

Harlequin Coffee Table (cont.)

5. Paint the diamonds and triangles with red, pink, green, turquoise, purple, teal, and mustard. Use Fig. B as a guide for color placement. To get clean lines, mask off alternating sections and paint. Remove tape. Let dry completely before taping over previously painted areas.

6. When all diamonds and triangles are dry, add dots where sections meet with white.

Painting the Legs:
See Fig. C & D for legs.

1. Transfer a smaller version of the vines to the top square areas of the legs. Paint these vines green using a small round brush.

2. Paint second sections of the legs with red. Let dry.

3. Draw an elongated diamond on each red section. See Fig. C. Mask off the diamonds. Paint diamonds with mustard, using a small flat brush, letting the brush strokes show.

4. Add dots around the tops of the red sections with turquoise.

5. Paint bands below red sections with purple. Let dry. Add dots with pink.

6. Paint sections below purple bands with green.

7. Paint bottom sections below green sections with black. Let dry.

8. Use a 1/4" flat brush to make white checks on bottom sections. (A brush this size makes squares about 1/2".)

Painting the Finials
See Fig. E.

1. Drill a hole in the bottom of each finial and a corresponding hole at the top of each leg. Insert one end of a double-ended screw in each finial.

2. Paint the finials with red, pink, green, turquoise, purple, teal, and mustard, randomly alternating colors for sections, dots, and stripes. Fig. E shows one color combination – the other finials are different placements of the same colors.

3. Use the same colors to paint the wooden wheels that go on the legs, alternating color placement for solid areas and dots.

Assembling & Finishing:

1. Drill holes for nails in the four sides of the legs at the centers of the mustard diamonds.

2. Nail the wooden wheels at the centers of the mustard diamonds on all sides of the legs.

3. Screw finials at the top of each leg.

4. Spray table with several coats matte sealer. Let dry between coats. ❑

Sponging

Sponging – creating a texture or pattern on a surface with a sponge – can be done randomly for a textured look or with sponge shapes to create a pattern. Variations in the sponge create variations in the effect. Natural sea sponges are most often used for textures; cellulose kitchen sponges can be easily cut with scissors to make shapes for sponged patterns. You can also tear the edges of a cellulose sponge to create an irregular shape that can be used for sponging textures. Both types of sponges may be purchased attached to mitts that can be used to create a variety of textures. Find them at hardware and crafts stores. To create transparent sponged effects, mix the paint with an equal amount of neutral glazing medium.

BASIC SUPPLIES

- Sponge – use either a sea sponge or a cellulose sponge, depending upon technique
- Latex paint, or acrylic paint, two (or more) colors
- Disposable foam or plastic plates, or paint tray, or palette

HERE'S HOW

1. Base paint the surface. Let dry.
2. Dampen sponge. Squeeze out excess water. Blot on a towel. The sponge should be damp and pliable, but not wet.
3. Pour paint for sponging on a plate or into a paint tray. Press sponge into paint to load. Blot the loaded sponge on a clean disposable plate or a clean part of the paint tray to distribute the paint.
4. Pounce the sponge on the surface, slightly overlapping each application to create texture (**photo 1** *or* pressing the sponge in a uniform way to create a pattern (**photo 3**).
   - To make crisp impressions, don't rub or drag the sponge.
   - To keep sponging from getting too dense, don't overwork the surface – pounce and move on.
   - To avoid a repeated texture, don't keep the sponge in the same position every time you touch the surface.

Random Sponging

Photo 1. Using a sea sponge to create a textured metallic look.

Photo 2. Sponged area of a chest.

Patterned Sponging

Photo 3. Using a small square cut from a sponge to create a pattern.

Photo 4. Patterned area of a serving cart.

SPONGED METALLIC CHEST OF DRAWERS

Created by Kirsten Jones

SUPPLIES

Furniture Piece:
Wooden cabinet with small drawers

Acrylic Paint:
Antique copper metallic
Bronze metallic
Gold metallic
Light blue-green

Tools & Other Supplies:
Old toothbrush
Sea sponge
Masking tape, 1"
1" brush
Sandpaper, 100 and 220 grit
Matte spray sealer

INSTRUCTIONS

Preparation & Base Painting:
1. Remove drawer pulls. Prepare cabinet, following instructions in the "Furniture Preparation" section.
2. Base paint top, sides, and drawer fronts of cabinet with antique copper metallic.
3. Base paint trim around top and base, area around drawers, and drawer pulls with light blue-green. Let dry.

Sponging:
1. Use tape to mask off areas painted with light blue-green.
2. Lightly sponge bronze metallic on areas painted with antique copper. Let dry.
3. Using an old toothbrush, spatter bronze-sponged areas with gold metallic.

Distressing:
1. Remove tape from areas painted with light blue-green. Sand these areas and the drawer pulls to create a distressed look.
2. Dilute antique copper metallic paint with water to make a wash. Brush diluted paint over light blue-green areas, including drawer pulls. Let dry.

Finishing:
1. Replace drawer pulls.
2. Spray with matte sealer. ❏

MOSAIC SERVING CART

Created by Kathi Bailey

*This dreary old 70's serving cart has seen better days, but it has a whole new life now.
The metal frame was spray painted bright white, and a stamped design in bright colors,
created with shapes cut from cellulose kitchen sponges, gives the trays of the cart a mosaic
look without the weight, bulk, or expense of ceramic tile.*

SUPPLIES

Furniture Piece:
Metal serving cart with removable
    trays

Paint:
Spray paint for metal surfaces - taupe,
    white
Gloss enamel acrylic craft paint
    (2 oz. bottles)
    Black
    Bright blue
    Orange
    White
    Yellow

Tools & Other Supplies:
Cellulose kitchen sponges
Charcoal pencil
Scissors
Paper palette
Water basin
Sponge brush

Pattern on page 125

INSTRUCTIONS

Preparation:
See pattern on page 125.
1. Remove trays from cart. Clean metal trays and base to remove dirt and loose
   paint.
2. Spray base with two coats white paint. Let dry 30 minutes between coats.
3. Spray trays with two coats taupe paint. Let dry 30 minutes between coats. Let
   second coat dry completely.
4. Paint edges of trays with black gloss enamel. Let dry.
5. Trace pattern onto tracing paper. Enlarge to fit your serving cart.
6. Transfer pattern to the top and bottom trays.

Sponging:
1. Cut dry cellulose sponges into five 3/4" squares (one for each gloss enamel color).
   Cut three more 3/4" squares and cut each into two triangles. Don't discard
   remaining sponge pieces – you'll use them later to cut smaller pieces to fill gaps.
2. Dampen all the sponges.
3. Pour a small amount of bright blue paint on a palette. Dip square sponge in
   paint and lightly press in four corners of each tray. Sponge a blue border around
   the edge of each tray, reloading sponge as needed. Rinse sponge.
4. Using a new square sponge, fill in the space around the flowers on two trays with
   stamped white squares, working from
   the outside in. Use photo as a guide.
5. On one tray, stamp flower petals with
   yellow, using triangles and squares.
6. On second tray, stamp flower petals
   with orange, using triangles and
   squares.
7. Fill in flower centers with Black.
8. On third tray, stamp the background
   with white squares and the rectangle
   in the center with black. (The rectangle pictured is nine squares wide
   and twelve squares long – adjust the
   size to fit your tray.) Let cure 48
   hours before using. ❑

Before sponging

Stamping

Stamping is a quick, easy way to create repeated motifs or a handpainted look. Stamping can be done with rubber stamps, pre-cut foam stamps, or printing blocks, which come in a wide variety of designs and sizes. You can also cut your own stamps from wood, vegetables, sponges, or dense foam stamp material. Acrylic craft paint or colored paint glaze, a translucent medium with a gel-like consistency, can be used for stamping. It's a good idea to practice stamping on a piece of poster board or paper before stamping your project.

BASIC SUPPLIES

- Rubber stamps, foam stamps, or printing blocks
- Acrylic craft paint or colored paint glaze
- Brushes for loading stamps with paint – foam brushes or foam wedges for rubber stamps and foam stamps, a flat bristle brush for printing blocks

HERE'S HOW

1. Load stamp with paint, using a brush. Be careful not to get paint in the crevices of the stamp.
2. Press stamp on surface, being careful not to slide the stamp.
3. Lift.

Rubber Stamps

Photo 1 - Pressing a rubber stamp on the surface.

Photo 2 - Lifting the stamp to reveal the image.

Foam Stamps

Photo 1 - Loading a foam stamp with paint, using a foam brush.

Photo 2 - Pressing the stamp to the surface.

Printing Blocks

Photo 3 - Blended paint colors on a printing block. Use a flat bristle brush for loading; blend before stamping.

Photo 4 - Lifting the printing block by the handle to reveal an image.

A PAIR OF PEAR CHAIRS

Created by Kathi Bailey

After a distressed finish was created on these chairs, the backs of the chairs were stamped with a pear motif in gold paint. A matching fabric was created for the chair seats by using the same pear stamp to stamp a spaced, repeated design on a short-napped upholstery fabric with brown paint.

SUPPLIES

Furniture Pieces:
Wooden chairs with upholstered seats

Acrylic Paint:
Brown
Gold metallic

Tools & Other Supplies:
Metal chain
Sandpaper - 100 grit, 220 grit
Stamp with pear motif
Solid color fabric (enough to cover both seats)
Furniture oil
Staple gun
Scissors
Disappearing fabric marker
Rubbing alcohol
Cloth rags
Tack cloth

INSTRUCTIONS

Preparation:
1. Remove seats from chairs. Remove fabric from seats.
2. Clean wood to remove dirt and grime.
3. Dampen rag with alcohol and rub over each chair to dull finish.
4. Cut fabric to fit chair seats.

Distressing:
1. Beat chairs with metal chain to distress wood.
2. Using 100 grit sandpaper, hand sand edges, corners, and legs of chairs where wear would most commonly occur. Sand down to bare wood in some spots – corners are a good choice.
3. Repeat sanding with 220 grit sandpaper.
4. Wipe chairs with a tack rag.
5. Dampen a rag with furniture oil and lightly rub over chair to restore sheen. Repeat, if needed, in heavily sanded areas.

Stamping:
1. Stamp chair backs on front and back with pear stamp, using gold metallic paint. Let dry.
2. Mark placement for pears on fabric, using photo as a guide.
3. Stamp pears on fabric with brown paint. Let dry.

Finishing:
Cover chair seats with fabric, following instructions for "Mix & Match Dining Chairs." ❏

STAMPED BEE CHAIR

Created by Kirsten Jones

The bee stamp and bee-patterned fabric were the inspiration for this chair.
Painted trim highlights the chair's lines. The colors for the trim were chosen to
complement the fabric.

SUPPLIES

Furniture Piece:
Wooden chair

Acrylic Paint:
Black
Gold metallic
Olive green
Pearl white metallic
Red
Sunflower yellow

Paint Brushes:
Round - #8 round
Flats - #10, 3/4"

Tools & Other Supplies:
Foam stamp with bee motif
Staple gun
Red fabric with gold bees (enough to
    cover chair seat)
Old toothbrush
Gloss spray sealer

INSTRUCTIONS

Preparation & Base Painting:
1. Remove chair seat. Prepare chair according to instructions in the "Furniture Preparation" section.
2. Base paint entire chair with black. Let dry.

Painting the Trim:
1. Paint leg stringers with olive green.
2. Trim edge of chair back with red, using a #10 flat brush.
3. Add a thin line of olive green inside red border, using a #8 round brush.

Stamping:
Stamp bee on back of chair, using pearl white metallic on wings and sunflower yellow and gold metallic on body. Let dry.

Finishing:
1. Spatter chair with gold metallic, using an old toothbrush. Let dry.
2. Spray with gloss sealer. Let dry completely.
3. Cover chair seat with fabric, following instructions for "Mix & Match Dining Chairs." ❑

Stenciling

Stenciling is a centuries-old decorative technique for adding painted designs to surfaces in which paint is applied through the cutout areas of a paint-resistant material.

Stencils are available at crafts and home improvement stores in a huge array of pre-cut designs. You can also buy stencil blank material and cut your own stencils with a craft knife.

A variety of paints can be used for stenciling, including acrylic craft paint, spray paint, stencil gels (gel-like paints that produce a transparent, watercolor look), and cream stencil paints. The paints can be applied with bristle stencil brushes, small paint rollers, or sponge brushes (round foam sponges on a handle). It's good to have several sizes of brushes — the size of the brush to use is determined by the size of the stencil opening.

BASIC SUPPLIES

• Stencils
• Paint, stencil paint or acrylic paint
• Brushes for stenciling
• Disposable plate or palette

HERE'S HOW

1. Pour some paint on a plate or palette. Holding the stencil brush perpendicular to the plate, dip the tips of the bristles in paint. (**photo 1**)
2. Lightly pounce the brush on a paper towel to remove excess paint. (**photo 2**)
3. Using a pouncing motion (**photo 4**) or a light circular stroke (known as the sweeping stroke) (**photo 3**), apply paint to the surface through the openings of the stencil. Use more pressure to create a darker print.

Photo 1 - Loading the brush.

Photo 2 - Pouncing brush on paper towel to remove excess paint.

Photo 3 - Stenciling by moving the brush in a circular motion, called a sweeping stroke, beginning on outside edge.

Photo 4 - Stenciling by pouncing the brush up and down.

FLOWERS & BUGS TABLE & CHAIRS

Created by Kathi Peterson

This cheery children's table and chairs is painted with bright primary colors, decorated with a freehand basketweave design painted with white, and stenciled with colorful flowers, dragonflies, and ladybugs. Adding a bit of outlining to the stenciled flowers and bugs makes them look handpainted rather than stenciled.

SUPPLIES

Furniture Pieces:
Children's table and chairs

Acrylic Paints:
Black
Blue
Green
Orange
Red
White
Yellow
You'll need 16 to 18 oz. of yellow paint, less of the other colors.

Artist's Paint Brushes:
Flats - 3/4", #12, #6, #2
Script liners - #2, #1

Stencils:
Pre-cut stencils with flower and bug motifs

Tools & Other Supplies:
Sponge brushes
Stencil brushes
Waterbase varnish

INSTRUCTIONS

Preparation:
Prepare table and chairs for painting, following instructions in the "Furniture Preparation" section.

Painting:
1. Base paint table and chairs, using sponge brushes and yellow paint. Let dry.
2. Using a script liner brush with white paint, paint basketweave design on tabletop and table legs and on chair seats, legs, spindles, and backs. Let dry.
3. Using a sponge brush, paint a blue band around the rim of table and the chair seats and backs. With a smaller round brush, paint blue rings on all legs and spindles. Touch up with small liner brush. Paint table supports blue. Let dry.
4. Using a flat brush, paint white line around blue lines. Let dry.
5. Using a stencil brush, paint white dots on blue lines. Let dry.
6. Using a round brush, paint a squiggle line around the perimeter of the table and chair seats.

Stenciling:
1. To create backgrounds and undercoats for the stenciled flowers and bugs, stencil the motifs with white paint on the chairs and table, using the photo as a guide for placement.
2. Create the white borders for the stenciled designs by painting around them with a brush to enlarge the motifs approximately 1/4" on all sides. Paint white lines for bug trails. Let dry.
3. Stencil with colors over the white backgrounds, using these colors:
   Dragonflies - blue and green
   Ladybugs - red
   Flowers - red, blue, green, and orange
   Let dry.

Finishing:
1. Using a liner brush, loosely outline each stencil with black paint. Paint broken black lines on bug trails. Let dry.
2. Paint black dots on ladybugs. Let dry.
3. Seal all painted surfaces with waterbase varnish. Let dry. ❏

FRENCH BENCH

Created by Kirsten Jones

A visit to France was the inspiration for this stenciled piano bench. Two stencils were used – one with a fleur-de-lis motif for the spaced, repeated design on the top, another with letters of the alphabet for spelling the names of French cities, stenciled around the apron. The black and gold color scheme is simple, dramatic, and elegant.

SUPPLIES

Furniture Piece:
Wooden piano bench

Acrylic Paint:
Black
Metallic gold

Stencils:
Alphabet stencil
Stencil with fleur-de-lis motif

Tools & Other Supplies:
Stencil brushes, 3/8", 1/2"
Flat brushes - 1", #12
Pencil
Ruler
Gloss spray sealer

Instructions follow on page 118.

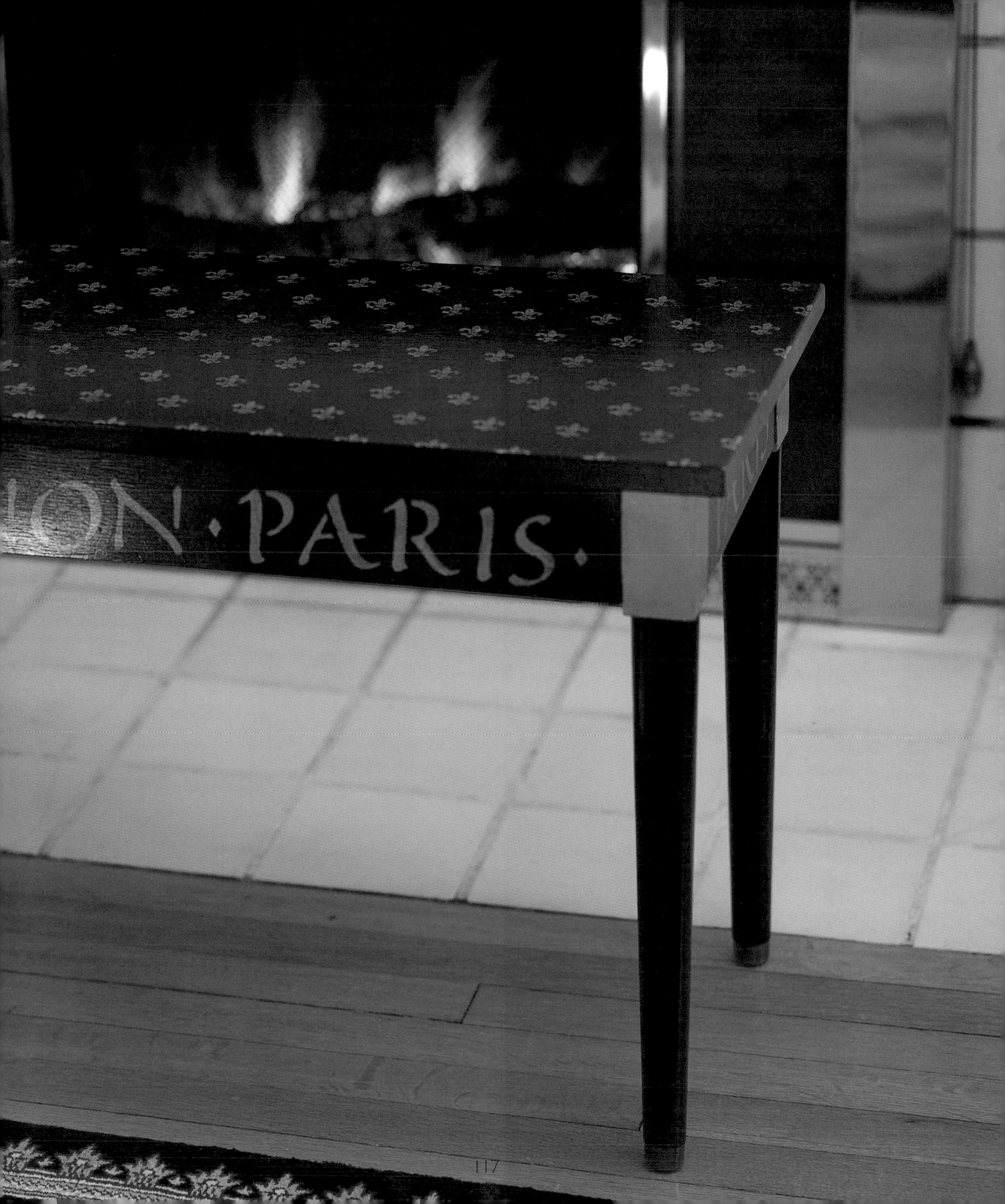
ION · PARIS ·

French Bench (cont.,)

INSTRUCTIONS

Preparation & Base Painting:
1. Prepare the bench for painting, following instructions in the "Furniture Preparation" section.
2. Base paint bench with two coats black. Let dry between coats.
3. Paint top of each leg with metallic gold. Let dry.

Stenciling:
1. Stencil names of French cities around apron of bench with metallic gold paint, using a 1/2" stencil brush.
2. With a pencil, mark placement of fleur-de-lis motifs. (These were spaced 2" apart on centers.)
3. Stencil fleur-de-lis motifs on top of bench with metallic gold, using a 3/8" stencil brush. Let dry.

Finishing:
Spray with several coats gloss sealer. Let dry between coats.

Hydrangea Console Table

Created by Kirsten Jones

Enjoy summer's hydrangeas all year long with this console table. Masking tape was used to create the subtly contrasting stripes on the top. The hydrangeas were stenciled the length of the table with stencil gels in greens, purple, and blue.

Supplies

Furniture Piece:
Wooden console table

Paint:
Acrylic paint - warm yellow, pale yellow
Stencil gels - ivy green, fern green, purple, light blue

Stencils:
Pre-cut stencil with hydrangea motifs

Tools & Other Supplies:
Masking tape, 1"
3/4" flat brush
Stencil brushes
Sandpaper, 220 grit
Tack cloth
Matte spray sealer

Instructions

Preparation & Base Painting:
1. Prepare table for painting, following instructions in the "Furniture Preparation" section.
2. Base paint tabletop with pale yellow. Let dry.
3. With masking tape, tape off 1" stripes on top of table. See photo for placement.
3. Paint stripes, table apron, and legs with warm yellow. Let dry.
4. Lightly sand table to soften stripes. Wipe away dust with a tack cloth.

Stenciling:
Stencil hydrangeas along center of tabletop, with stencil gels. Use photo as a guide for color placement. Let dry.

Finishing:
Spray with matte sealer. ❏

See project pictured on pages 120-121.

WICKER PLANT STAND

Created by Kirsten Jones

Spray paint also can be used for stenciling. Leaf motifs, cut from stencil blank material using pattern, decorate this wicker plant stand. Interior/exterior paint supplies a weather-resistant coating; use masking tape to shield the metal legs from overspray.

SUPPLIES

Furniture Piece:
Woven wicker plant stand with metal
  legs

Interior/Exterior Spray Paint:
Tan
Dark green
Light green

Stencils:
Stencil blank material, two
  8" x 10" sheets

Tools & Other Supplies:
Masking tape
Craft knife
Permanent felt-tip marker
Piece of glass with finished edges or
  self-healing cutting mat

INSTRUCTIONS

Preparation:
1. Tape off metal legs and base of plant stand to protect them from paint.
2. Spray all wicker areas with tan paint. Let dry completely.

Stenciling:
See pattern on pages 124.
1. Trace leaf design on stencil blank material with permanent marker.
2. Cut out stencil, using a craft knife, on glass or cutting mat.
3. Position stencil on plant stand, using photo as a guide for placement, and spray with light green paint. Let dry.
4. Add additional motifs with dark green spray paint. Let dry completely.

Finishing:
Remove masking tape from legs. ❑

Patterns for Wicker Plant Stand

Actual Size Pattern

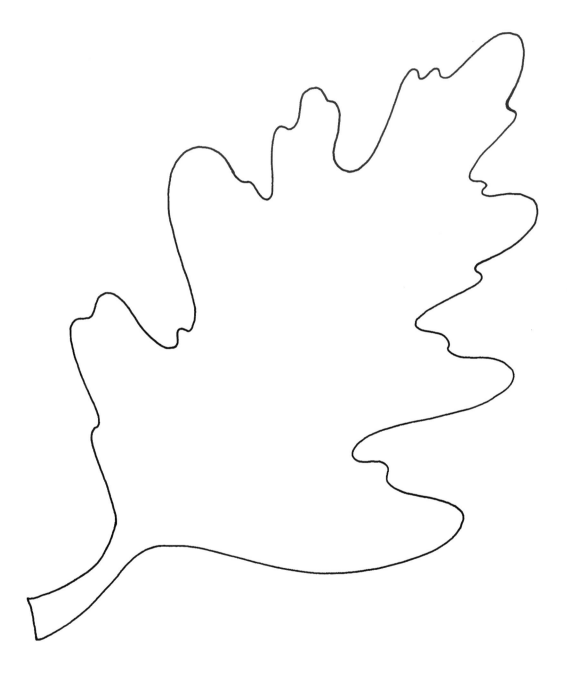

Pattern for Mosaic
Serving Cart

*Enlarge pattern @133%
for actual size.*

Pattern for Harlequin Coffee Table

Enlarge @118% for actual size.

See instructions on page 94.

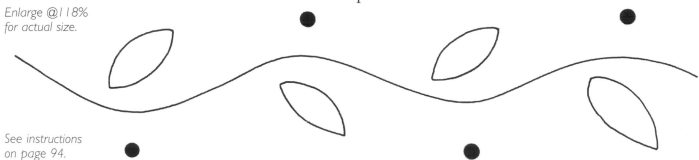

Pattern for Round Parlor Table – Actual Size

See instructions on page 66

METRIC CONVERSION CHART

Inches to Millimeters and Centimeters

Inches	MM	CM
1/8	3	.3
1/4	6	.6
3/8	10	1.0
1/2	13	1.3
5/8	16	1.6
3/4	19	1.9
7/8	22	2.2
1	25	2.5
1-1/4	32	3.2
1-1/2	38	3.8
1-3/4	44	4.4
2	51	5.1
3	76	7.6
4	102	10.2
5	127	12.7
6	152	15.2
7	178	17.8
8	203	20.3
9	229	22.9
10	254	25.4
11	279	27.9
12	305	30.5

Yards to Meters

Yards	Meters
1/8	.11
1/4	.23
3/8	.34
1/2	.46
5/8	.57
3/4	.69
7/8	.80
1	.91
2	1.83
3	2.74
4	3.66
5	4.57
6	5.49
7	6.40
8	7.32
9	8.23
10	9.14

INDEX

INDEX